SIMPLE AWAKENING

SIMPLE AWAKENING

The Power of Inner Silence

MICHAEL LINENBERGER

New Academy Publishers
Santa Fe, New Mexico

Published by New Academy Publishers: www.napubs.com
Distributed by NBN Books: www.nbnbooks.com

First printing 2016

ISBN: 978-0983364740
Library of Congress Control Number: 2016900016

Cover photograph by Faye and Patrick Bates: www.LightWorksMedia.biz
Cover design by Sarah Clarehart: www.sarahclarehart.com

CONTENTS

1.

Introduction to Simple Awakening

I'm sitting on a plane to San Francisco, returning home after giving one of my workday productivity seminars to the staff of a San Diego engineering firm. Here at thirty thousand feet, I've just finished taking a short session of "silence"—a *meditation* really. I've been taking these periods of inner silence nearly every morning and early evening for the last three years, but usually at ground level and usually in quiet and by myself. But today I ran out of time as I dashed to the airport, and I wanted to fit it in. It's been a while since I took silence with so many people around, so sitting here with my eyes closed is leading to an interesting thought: If I were to tell anyone here what I'm currently experiencing, they'd be amazed. Actually, it's more likely they'd just plain *disbelieve* me—or perhaps even dismiss me as a crank.

You see, I'm having yet another silence session that is filled with very sweet *bliss*. In nearly all my silence sessions every day now, a sweet and consistent sensation of bliss has started in my gut and has spread throughout my whole body. The best way to describe this bliss is that it's like sweet honey being poured through me and saturating my being. It's a pure and all-pervasive happiness experienced on all levels. Needless to say, it's very, very, nice.

BASED ON INNER SILENCE

More important, that bliss is rising from a profound presence of inner *silence*. That silence is on the one hand very *still* but on the other hand bubbling with subtle energy and insight. The inner silence connects and grounds me with what I can only call my highest good. Really, the silence feels as if it's the core of who I am—and at the same time, the core of everything else. Due to that silence, I feel profoundly expanded, incredibly whole, and deeply supported.

These experiences have been going on for almost three years now, increasing steadily over that time. As you can expect, they have gotten my attention! The silence is by far the most important and practical feature of this unfolding: it permeates and supports my whole day. As a result, my work—and life—have been deeply and dramatically transformed. I feel as if a rock-solid platform is supporting and facilitating my every move now, as nearly all actions I take are easy, effective, and satisfying. The presence of small fears and insecurities of the day, which in the past were typically either at or below the surface of my mind, have disappeared—they've been replaced with a consistent feeling of stability, grounding, and expansion. The sense of having too little time and too few resources to reach my work and life goals is gone.

Instead, a strong sensation of confidence, competence, and fulfillment sits in the background of my awareness at all times—it comes from that silence. Even my day-to-day work is much easier and more productive. As a result of all this, my life feels infinitely more satisfying. And along with all of this is the sweetness of that bliss—it's like frosting on a cake because, even when it only sits subtly in the background, it adds a consistent layer of fulfillment as I'm moving through life. All this continues to grow month by month as the silence grows.

What Is Simple Awakening?

What is this all about? In a moment, I'll explain what I found these experiences to be. I'll explain how the silence and the resulting bliss and spontaneous improvements in life are the early and very practical stages of awakening—*spiritual awakening,* in fact. But it's a very *simple* version of spiritual awakening, one that brings major improvements to all aspects of life, but without anything *weird.* This is not the spiritual awakening of the seventies with viewing auras, seeing bright white light, or communicating with spirits or deities. Rather, I have found that the establishment of deep supporting inner silence in my daily awareness is incredibly transformational without being "out there." Because of that, I call it *simple awakening.* The immense grounding and expansion that comes with deep silence is better than those unusual things anyway. It's simpler than that, sweeter than all that, and amazingly useful.

If I'm not meeting spirits, why do I call this *spiritual* awakening? You'll see as the book progresses that I feel this pure inner silence is the truest form of *spirit* and that the best definition of spiritual awakening is connecting to and stabilizing that blissful and expansive silence as an all-time reality in your awareness. Stabilizing silence in your awareness changes *everything.* All the qualities and characteristics of spirit come rushing into life: compassion, positivity, right action, curiosity, inclusiveness, broad insight, courage, peace, wisdom, openness, and so on all tumble into and dominate life. The negatives in life mostly drop away. Life just starts to work right and amazingly well.

In the chapters ahead, I'll talk about what these changes are and what this awakening means. I'll discuss where it comes from and how you, the reader, may be able to culture it as well. In fact, that's the purpose of this book: to convey to you, from a lay perspective, how transformational awakening to inner silence is and how *accessible* it is. I have found that it's not just for spiritual devotees, as many previously thought. I truly believe that more and more "normal" people can have and benefit from growing awakening. That's why I've decided to write this book—so that whether simple awakening happens spontaneously for you or whether you start some simple awakening practices to help it along, you can recognize and encourage the silence as it grows in you and then gain its benefits. But first, let me talk a bit more about how this came about and how it has so dramatically changed my life.

COMPLETELY UNEXPECTED

In a way, all this has come out of left field—completely unexpected. You see, I'm a business author and I own a publishing and seminar company. Before that, I was a vice president at the large management consulting firm Accenture. My business work has been and still is very down-to-earth stuff. Currently, I teach people how to be more efficient and productive at work, which is a pretty normal topic area.

However, these awakening experiences, while also very pragmatic, are anything *but* down-to-earth. Rather, they are amazing and far outside the norm. When these experiences started three years ago, I was not seeking them—I was not meditating at the time, doing any other practices, or even studying the topic of awakening. But the experiences came, and come they have, every day and often quite intensely: a deep, profound, and consistent silence supporting all of my life and that experience of sweet honey-like bliss.

In contrast, for the decade prior to this happening, I was in the typical situation of so many Westerners: overextended and not satisfied with life. I was working way too hard and keeping way too many hours, often including weekends, and my life in general was predominantly unfulfilled. I was doing what many busy people do: trying to find time after work periods when I could finally do fun and satisfying things with friends or family, with the goal of finding a balanced and happy life. But that was hard to do—with all there was to do to succeed at work, where was the time for me to enjoy my life? And where was the *meaning* in life? The grind of business and success seeking typically sucked the joy out of life.

TRYING TO CONTROL LIFE

The core problem seemed to be that even though I was doing everything I thought I should do to succeed and gaining lots of "things," I was never reaching the sense of satisfaction I wanted. No matter how hard I worked, how carefully I arranged my life, or how many things I bought, there was always something more I needed to be happy—and I couldn't be satisfied until that next thing was attained. Even when I did reach a distinct milestone of success—say, releasing a new book, securing a large contract, or affording a big purchase—the happiness was muted because I felt that I was giving too much to reach that success and not leaving enough of myself to appreciate it.

As I look back, I can see my approach was pretty typical of how most busy people approach work and life. I was trying to reach my intended outcomes solely through control, action, and smarts. If the result didn't come, I just worked harder. We all believe that if we work hard, life should reward us. If we're smart and make good decisions, life should unfold happily for us, right?

Well, I did try to work hard and cover all the right bases. And I did try to manage things intelligently. But I was finding that the more I tried to succeed by controlling and managing things, the more I had to *do* to affect what I was trying to control. The efforts seemed to expand exponentially as I identified every detail that needed attention. This gave me less time to do what I really wanted.

All this happened even though I had very good work processes in place. After all, I'm an expert on managing work tasks and managing communications—I write books on that topic—so I had mastered efficiency to a degree greater than nearly *anyone* possibly can. But even with that, I was working too hard and missing out on life. I longed for a richness and meaning in life. The meaning I thought I'd find in my business ventures, while fairly good, just wasn't adequate. My personal life on the surface looked complete—even enviable. I had a nice home on a golf course in a beautiful town in Northern California. On my time off, I golfed and as often as possible took drives in my convertible up and down the California coast, enjoying the magic of that state. And I had a wonderful partner who cared for me deeply, and I for her. But deep inside I still felt as if I weren't reaching what I wanted.

INNER SILENCE ARRIVES

All that transformed dramatically starting three years ago, and it has accelerated ever since. The solution did not have to do with changing my approach to work or life. I didn't find new and clever time-saving approaches, and I didn't force myself to take more time doing important activities. Rather, the solution came from deep inside, at first spontaneously and on its own accord and then with some encouragement from me. Inner silence started to creep into my life—and that changed everything.

The silence first appeared three years ago when I closed my eyes to say a silent grace at a Thanksgiving gathering. It was the first time in a long time that I closed my eyes with inner attention, and I suddenly found my awareness dropping into a deep field of inner silence. It was utterly quiet and completely still, with a sense of infinite breadth to it. I sensed I was on another plane of awareness. I thought to myself afterward, *Wow, that was interesting.* In the days ahead, I couldn't get my mind off the experience, and I made a point of closing my eyes with inner attention as often as I could to repeat the experience—and it did repeat.

This wasn't my first brush with a meditation-style activity. I'd meditated years ago and at that time studied it and the concept of awakening a fair amount. But after a while with no awakening results, I'd stopped and dismissed awakening as something not possible for me. Nonetheless, my study during those early years taught me what awakening was *supposed* to look like, and that served me well as this new experience of silence arrived—it was clear it could be part of an awakening process.

That encouraged me to immediately start taking regular silence sessions again and to start reading about spiritual awakening again. With daily silence sessions over several weeks and months, the silence increased. I embraced it and allowed it to grow, and now, three years later, it has expanded to the point that it can be called an authentic expression of spiritual awakening—with tons of related benefits. I can say now with certainty that spiritual awakening is real.

One goal for this book is to help you to recognize inner silence as it arrives in your life. If you get even a small sense of it, I want to encourage you to embrace it and accept its arrival in your life. It could be the start of a similar awakening experience for you. If you don't embrace it at its early stages, if you dismiss it and don't put a little time aside each day to culture that inner silence, you could be pushing out the very key to your happiness.

THE VALUE OF SILENCE

Inner silence is an amazing thing. We often hear from many different sources about the deep treasures of finding or taking silence—and those praises are all true! In nearly every culture, religion, and philosophy, inner silence is accepted as noble and refined, and as an extremely important thing, as it should be—it *is* noble.

Think about the common ways we all pay homage to silence. When we want to show respect for a loss, we take a moment of inner silence. When we want to bring order back to a chaotic discussion, we encourage a moment of silence. Those who rise above the mundane world in silent contemplation are deeply admired. In church, in study, and in intimate moments, silence is revered as sacred and deeply connecting.

The phrase "Silence is golden" is actually quite an accurate statement because there *is* immense treasure in silence. If you look around, you'll see that the best things in our world ultimately emerge from silence. Study any of the ancient religions or philosophies and you'll see that silence is the starting point from which many if not most spiritual insights emerge. Nearly all religions and philosophies have reference after reference to how important silence is to happiness and to connecting with the highest aspects of life.

In all walks of life, you'll hear stories of how silence can guide your life—you're told to trust "the still, small voice within." You're advised to look silently within to find the insights you need for correct action in life. Many of us know that is true—many of us find our best decisions come when we look silently inward. Many of us have experienced the peace and stability that comes from taking short silent periods or even days-long retreats into silence, whether in organized sessions or through simple retreats into nature. And many of us know how crucial such periods are to supporting our later busy periods.

SILENCE EMERGES AS A PRESENCE

So inner silence, at even a basic level, is worthy of achieving. But when inner silence emerges deeply and profoundly as the first stages of awakening, it's *life changing*, as this book will show. Furthermore, it's important to note that inner silence is not so much *imposed* as it is *accepted*. When the right conditions are engaged, inner silence emerges on its own, as a profound presence. When I take a silence session these days, I don't try to push out thoughts or images or noises. Rather, I just create the appropriate inner conditions, and then silence comes in powerfully, on its own, and clears everything from its path in an amazing way.

Later you'll find that it's not just during a closed-eyes session that silence emerges. Early on after taking regular silence sessions, I found that with time and just a little practice, inner silence even persisted into my awareness *all day long*, right into the busy activity of my day, with remarkable outcomes. Currently, that silence is an all-time experience underlying every moment of my life. I now see that such silence is at the basis of my entire being and *everyone's* being; whether we sense it or not, it's at the basis of who we really are. It's at the *core* of life—we merely need to awaken to that.

Silence is not just at the core of human life, but it's also at the core of all of nature itself. Silence is everywhere in nature. Think about it: It's no mistake that silence is the thing you sense most when you're in pure and pristine locations in nature. The silence of a quiet mountain lake at dusk, the peacefulness of a silent sunset, the magic of soundless falling snow, the quiet pauses between the laps of water up onto a beach.

Paradoxically, silence is also at the basis of nature's noisiest and most dynamic expressions. Just as a wave emerges from a silent ocean to create the thunder of surf, silence is the underlying field from which all the most energetic aspects of nature and our life emerge. *All* the expressions of our manifest reality, from the quiet to the explosive, are the results of vibrations in the infinite field of invisible silence.

It makes sense that tapping into that silence and living from it can greatly improve and transform our lives. Spiritual awakening is the realization that that field rests inside us all and that we can bring it to the surface where we can benefit immensely from it. When profound inner silence permeates all your activity, you gain deep insight, wisdom, and the ultimate bliss of knowing all is well.

PRACTICAL AND GUIDED

So silence—especially inner silence, if accepted—can be an insightful and beautiful thing. When silence is growing in your all-day consciousness in awakening, it's also an incredibly *practical* thing. That's because, with awakening, the ever-present silence firmly supports your daily activities. It serves as a rock-solid foundation for action. It provides the basis for clear, insightful, and meaningful thinking. It intuitively guides you throughout your day to your most valuable actions. And it brings you calm and collected results.

That's exactly what I found. Slowly but surely, with the gradual growth of silence becoming permanently present in my awareness over the last years, I found my decisions getting better, my work getting easier, and my life reaching more accomplishments—ones with a lot more meaning. As silence grew more and more, I found myself enjoying work and life more and found the heaviness of life lifting off my shoulders. I soon found that my struggles in work and life were disappearing; rather, my work and personal actions started coming easily. There were no more feelings of being behind on things or missing out—work and life grew to become a consistent pleasure.

A question I often get at this point when describing my transformation is this: "But even if I gain inner silence, don't I still have to do all the many things I need to do to support my family and my style of living? How does just *feeling* better with more silence accomplish all those things?" My answer is that awakening to inner silence is not just a matter of *feeling* better. It's a matter of spontaneously living and working better. I get way more done in much less time because I spin my wheels much less often.

Think of all the things you do in work and life that don't pan out, that end up being unnecessary or even down right wrong. With silence being consistently present, it seems now as if I'm being *guided* by that silence, that wholeness. It seems as if the silence is *leading* me to just the right next steps to accomplish the things I need with less effort and less time.

I know that may sound crazy to you, my claim that silence can actually guide you to your best outcomes, but that's exactly what's happening—so much so that these days, I rarely have questions as to what to do next in my personal or business life—the wisdom of the best next step is nearly always there. As a result, actions seem easy and simple even in the midst of my normally very busy business day. I don't waste time, and my actions seem more and more to lead to the right outcomes. Business deals (the right ones) are closing with less effort, sometimes seemingly out of the blue, since I'm guided to the right decisions at the right times. All aspects of life are easier and more effective.

Pragmatic Awakening

These and many more very positive things are going on in my life as a result of this simple awakening to silence. I summarize much of that below and describe it in more detail later in the book. But let's step back a moment and talk about what the heck is going on. I'm not complaining, obviously, but what is this awakening to silence and why is it happening?

After some research, I've come to learn more about this onset of silence, bliss, and internal guidance—this thing that I feel can be called a simple and powerful form of spiritual awakening. As I stated earlier, the concept of awakening is not new to me. I studied theories of spiritual awakening in my younger years. I even meditated twice a day consistently for several decades, looking for more peace and happiness, and admittedly hoping to experience *some* sort of awakening—at least as it was defined in those days.

But back in the seventies, when I first read about spiritual awakening, it was described as quite an exotic thing. It was portrayed as a life-rocking experience in which the meaning of life was suddenly dropped into your awareness and you were instantly transformed into a mystical being. In most cases, the awakened ones that got attention came from India or Asia; they walked around in robes and sandals and looked very different from you and me. These were the gurus and teachers of Eastern religions and philosophies, and they attracted many followers, including many people I knew.

Over time, however, I noticed that those who followed them did not seem to achieve any sort of awakening status. While many got some small and healthy benefits, decades passed with no life-transforming breakthroughs. None of my meditating peers seemed to be near the sort of awakening they aspired to; I never heard stories from meditator friends saying they or others they knew had reached it. Rather, the ongoing stories of awakening were still told by only a very select few, usually people who had adopted a very spiritual life—not people like you and me.

And so years ago I gave up on the idea that such an awakening was attainable. I'd decided that awakening, if it even existed, was a supernatural thing reserved only for a few exceptionally devoted people—that it was *very* rare. I decided that it was certainly not attainable by people like me, who were completely immersed in the business and material world.

Fast-forward to the last three years, and significant awakening experiences have in fact been arriving for me—at first just a little and then much more. Initially, I rejected spiritual awakening as the probable explanation for the growing inner experiences that were bringing me so many benefits. My experiences were not that mystical. While they were very profound, they were just too *simple*. Surely, awakening had to be more flashy than simply problems falling away, sweetness flowing in, intuition guided me, and a very satisfying sense of freedom and stability moving in. Didn't it need to come with a set of "cosmic" experiences?

Awakening *Is* Very Simple

But as my experiences grew, I realized that the essence of spiritual awakening *is* very simple—it's not necessarily the glamorous supernatural transformation that I'd heard about in the seventies. Rather, I now know that at least one form of spiritual awakening is simply profound inner silence, inner stillness, and inner guidance taking hold and fully transforming your life. And I now know that it can happen without the trappings or requirements of an Eastern (or Western) spiritual lifestyle, which I had long assumed was a necessity.

And even though it's immensely simple, there *are* amazing aspects to awakening. That's because the silence and bliss *do* take on nearly super-natural levels as they transform your entire life. For example, the sense and reality of freedom from life's mundane limitations is totally amaz-ing—as is the ease that permeates life as each next step in life is guided by intuition.

But still I think awakening is better viewed through very pragmatic eyes, as to how life improves in *practical* ways as a result of those under-lying changes. My goal for decades has been to help people to solve their everyday problems, and that goal has not changed. While many people may be attracted by descriptions of silence and bliss, I still believe it's the positive effects of awakening on everyday mundane life that *most* people are looking for.

When I talk to people in the work world about what they need most, the majority focus simply on improving their daily life. While many peo-ple list specific and sometimes lofty life goals they want to achieve, most simply say they want relief from the problems and headaches of life. A number of people list specific health issues they want solved—relief from such issues is really all those people want from life. A vast majority say they want freedom from overwhelm—they describe the same over-taxed life that I described for myself prior to awakening, and they just want to get ahead of that and perhaps find at least a *little* more meaning in life beyond merely chasing success.

The beauty of this simple form of spiritual awakening is that all those pragmatic things are exactly what you get—all of them! For example,

I've already mentioned how my actions in my business and personal life are much easier and more effective. I'm finding that my life goals are simplifying and falling into place much more easily. My mind is amazingly clear and sharp but relaxed at the same time, and that leads to solutions to innumerable small problems coming easily. I'm even sensing, more and more, the ultimate outcomes of choices before they happen, so I'm making decisions much more accurately that unfold in a positive way. Most of my health issues have diminished or disappeared—I can see now that they were mostly stress related, and stress is definitely gone. And those issues that haven't disappeared don't seem to bother me as much now.

EXPERIENCING LIFE MORE FULLY

Really, the key is that nearly all my problems and dissatisfactions in life are dropping away, and that frees up space to live my life more and more completely. I enjoy all aspects of life many times more as a deep richness in life sets in with less of the internal filtering that often prevented me from enjoying life fully.

We all filter our experiences in ways that limit our lives. For example, the judgmental dialog that used to be in the back of my mind saying "this is bad to consume," or "that is good to do," or "I shouldn't do that," or "I should be sure to avoid this other thing"—all the *controls* I tried to place on life to try to *manipulate* my reality—those are gone. And that's good because those controls never really worked anyway, and they just prevented me from living spontaneously. Instead, I now experience life simply, mostly nonjudgmentally, and joyfully; I'm seeing and enjoying the richness that life naturally has. And right action—even *moral* action—seems to be coming on its own rather than through constant control.

I'm also having the most amazing personal insights about people—for example, about what motivates people, why most people usually end up unhappy, and how such unhappiness is ultimately unnecessary. The Buddha said awakening *ends suffering*, and I'm seeing what he meant by that because so far for me, awakening is setting life up to be an incredibly insightful and joyful experience.

BUSINESS PRACTICALITY

Long before awakening set in for me, I had been teaching workday management solutions, so it's amazing for me to see how, with growing silence, positive outcomes in business and work are now appearing almost automatically, along with a deep sense of fulfillment. So from a purely business point of view, it goes without saying that this experience, this state of being I'm describing, is *very* important. It's a hundred times more important than just becoming more efficient at what I do.

No, it's a thousand times more important than that. And in a way it's the ultimate *level* of workday management. After all, imagine if work were no longer a struggle. Imagine if nearly all your tasks in work and life were accurately falling into place and getting done effortlessly, even blissfully. Imagine if instead of going home feeling tired and frustrated each workday, you went home fulfilled. What if I could teach you *that*?

So I'm also realizing that this awakening, for me, may be an incredible *responsibility*. As a writer and communicator—as a teacher who shows people how to improve their work lives—it's becoming clear to me that I have to spread the word on this. I'm not being given this gift so I can go out and just make more money or sit back and soak in the bliss. I know I need to do much more than that. In fact, since it has such huge implications for the quality of work life, this is probably the logical next step for my current line of teaching. This book, then, is the first step of that.

SHOULD I BE WRITING ABOUT AWAKENING?

However, this book on awakening is a big departure for me. Previous to writing this book, I was a *business* writer. I've written seven books on workday productivity, and my primary day-to-day business was to give seminars on that topic. Prior to those activities, I was deeply imbedded in the corporate world. As I said, I was a VP and management consultant at Accenture. Before that I had various IT management roles in the software industry and in government, and years ago I even had a career as a civil engineer. My current activity of writing and teaching my system of task and e-mail management has been quite successful, and some of my books on the topics have even become best sellers in their categories. Clearly, I have a well-established career. And so the question is, should I switch gears and start writing about awakening? Isn't that a bit crazy?

Well, yes, maybe it is crazy. But you see, even though it seems like awakening is a risky topic for me, there's no doubt in my mind that this book is needed. I have now come to deeply believe that awakening is a real possibility for many, many people—even people who've never considered it before. And so I feel a book like this, one that presents awakening in a way that even a business person might accept, will help a lot of people who may never learn about it otherwise. Everyone—whether they be monks, artists, public servants, or people in the business world—should have a way to access this information.

I have recently concluded that a life dedicated to spiritual pursuit is *not* necessary to reach awakening. I wasn't on a spiritual or new age path at the time awakening hit me; rather, I was focused on my business. So I've written this book in a very practical and I hope *believable* way—in a way that I hope will convince almost anyone that *awakening is real*, and that it's even possible for them.

SUMMARY OF PRACTICAL BENEFITS OF AWAKENING TO SILENCE

That's my story of what has led up to writing this book and how in general it has benefited me. In the chapters ahead, I'll give many more details.

But again, I want to emphasize that while awakening was in the past mostly shrouded in mystery and linked with esoteric pursuits, it doesn't have to be that way. It is really a hugely accessible and practical thing. Let me summarize many of the bottom-line benefits of what I'm experiencing with the onset of awakening to silence:

I'm happier than I've ever been, and that affects both work and life. But it's not happiness like one feels when getting a new car or having fun with friends or reaching a life or business goal. Rather, my happiness is not *conditional* on having certain things or taking certain actions—happiness is just there, nearly always. It's a deep-level contentment permeating *all* aspects of life.

There is nothing out of sorts in my life; rather, everything feels (and is) in balance. I have a deep knowing that all is well and that I'm on a perfect work-and-life path. I no longer have lingering suspicions that I should be working on something else, approaching life differently, or seeking other activities or other sources of income.

Life has gotten very easy. Work is easy, day-to-day relationships are easy, and moving through all the functions of life is easy. I don't mean that I'm taking on only easy work and avoiding challenges. No, I'm still accomplishing all I did before and more—but doing it now is just very easy. I have a wonderful sense of *freedom*, as if work and life are no longer constraining me.

All sense of self-doubt and fear have left. I have no fears in social or business situations. I no longer have the feeling that I have to prove myself to anyone. And most significantly perhaps, I have no *money* fears (even though I don't have a tremendous amount in the bank). I'm confident the money will be there when I need it—and for a businessman, that's amazing. And I even no longer have a fear of death. It's as if a profound sense of completeness has set in.

I now have very little striving. In the past, I was constantly trying to get to the next big thing that I had to reach for (whatever it was at that moment) and not quite getting there. So I tried even harder each time. *Striving* is the perfect word for that. In the past, I had a nearly constant internal conversation that went like this: "Once I get X, I'll be happy." This led to my striving for X. The item X could be a big goal like the next big sale, or the next job, or the next big purchase. Or it could be a simple short-term goal like wanting to arrive at my destination when driving across town. In all these cases, I was constantly living with the next milestone being necessary for my happiness or completeness. Of course, that milestone was consistently around the corner and just out of reach. And once I reached it, there would be another one just beyond it to attend to. In other words, I was constantly striving for some later attainment, living for the future, and never quite reaching it. But now that striving has gone away, I'm mostly living in the now, taking life for what it offers and spontaneously appreciating it unconditionally as I move ahead.

I'm more motivated about work and life than I have ever been before. That's somewhat paradoxical, given how content I am in my current status. But no, I now have a deeper sense of inner purpose, and it motivates all that I do. But rather than working from fear or an itch to fill an incompleteness or even from the need to win, I'm working with a knowing that my actions are important and beneficial to others, and that I want to do even more to help.

I have a deep knowing that whatever I need next in life will appear when it's needed. That confidence is there partly because I'm regularly experiencing that. And it's there partly because my life has become very simple—I don't feel as if I have huge needs that I have to hustle for anymore. I still have big *goals*, perhaps even *bigger* now, but they aren't so much for *me* anymore, and they're much less material focused.

I now have a very powerful and effective *intuition*, one that I deeply trust. That is perhaps the most important of all these points. Because of that reliable intuition, decisions are very easy; I look inside and the answers come—answers that seem to nearly always be the right ones.

So that's my list. And there are a lot more things I could point to. I could describe each item on this list much more deeply. For many items, I *will* do that—I will elaborate on them later in the book. Many of these points also beg for a deeper, almost *philosophical* discussion. After all, much of what I just listed are topics that have been debated by deep thinkers throughout the ages. I'll try to identify and wade into those philosophical points as well, but from a very practical and personal perspective. I'm not aiming for any literary awards here, and I think you'll like how I explain these ahead.

In Closing

That's my experience. It really is happening daily, and the experiences are increasing with each month. There's no doubt in my mind, however, that I have a long way to go. I know that while the silence and bliss in my life and the benefits they bring are a profound first level of awakening, *full* awakening is some ways off. Why do I think that?

Well, first of all, I've always heard that full awakening is a non-variable, consistent state. However, everything I describe above is somewhat changeable in its expression. There are times (admittedly rarer these days) when the awakening experiences seem to drop off somewhat, and there are times when those experiences flow in more strongly. But luckily, the dips are slight and the silence and bliss continue to expand month by month.

The other reason I sense there is more to awakening is this: In many writings, *full* awakening is associated with highly spiritual insights—seeing into the cosmos, perhaps understanding God, and so on. I know one awakened person who, when he closes his eyes, travels throughout the spiritual realms. But, I seem to be experiencing a much more practical level of awakening. And that's fine because the list of benefits I discussed above is nothing to scoff at! And if those greater things do come, I'll just write another book! But still, I recognize there's a huge range of experiences above the first levels of awakening.

Next in *this* book, I could continue to describe the results of my experience of simple awakening even more. But instead, in the following chapters I'd like first to talk about what I think this awakening really is and what it means. I've become a bit of an expert on it now, as I've studied it to figure out what is happening. I have a unique perspective in that I come from a business world where I'm still fully engaged. It's a down-to-earth and practical perspective, one that I think you and many others can relate to.

Here's how I've laid out the next parts of the book. In the next chapter, I'll talk about the early onset of silence that eventually led to what I call awakening—what that looked like for me when it first started, how you might recognize it in your life, and what I think it means. After that I'll discuss more profound silence and awakening experiences—what they were and why they're important. Then I'll discuss how *you* may be able to develop silence and awakening—what you can do to increase your chances of experiencing that. After that, I'll talk more about intuition and how it grows with awakening. Then I'll discuss the influence of awakening on work and business life—and a lot more! In all this writing, I'll try to link everything to practical aspects of life. And especially, at all times, I'm going to try to keep it *real*. So stay with me.

2.

THE ONSET OF DEEP INNER SILENCE

Let me tell you how it all started. In early September of 2014, I started a drive from California to Santa Fe, New Mexico, to spend a number of days writing there. I made the decision to take that trip in a rather spontaneous way. In fact, the abruptness of my decision to go surprised both me and my girlfriend; with almost no notice I decided to jump in my car and drive away for a week. On the way, I was still figuring out my trip—why was I doing it?

It definitely was a writing trip, that much was certain. I'd been trying to write my next book for some time, and I wasn't making the progress I'd hoped. I was writing *some*, but I kept discarding what I created because it didn't sound or feel right to me. Somehow, I reasoned, a different location would knock the right material loose. I'd been drawn to visit Santa Fe recently, for the first time in decades. But for some reason, I felt a distinct urgency around doing all that *immediately*, and that's why I was on the road for Santa Fe, with almost no planning.

Along the way, I also decided that while there, I would visit my old friend Lance Eaves—someone I hadn't seen or talked to in many years and who had reached out to me by e-mail months before. So I texted him on the way to say I was coming. Moments later, my cell phone rang and Lance told me that he would unfortunately be out of town for the first days I'd be there. But he said he'd be back soon and quickly added, "Hey, why don't you use my apartment before I get back—maybe you can write there."

And before he hung up, he blew me away with the following bit of information: In the casita-apartment complex where he lived, over fifty published books had been written across the previous decades, and the complex was known for having a nearly magical vibe that seemed to encourage successful writing. A large number of those books had been written right in the very unit Lance was in. So I was going to have two undisturbed days of writing in a supposedly magical writing location. Perhaps I *would* find the book solution I needed.

I arrived at my Santa Fe hotel late at the end of my second day of driving, and the next morning I immediately headed over to the complex. I discovered that his casita was located in a beautiful old section of Santa Fe, just off Canyon Road, which is the primary art studio and gallery section of Santa Fe. His casita apartment was one of those hundred-year-old adobe structures that occupy the historic sections of Santa Fe. It had thick, pink-brown, stucco-like adobe walls, turquoise-blue woodwork around the doors and windows, and exposed hand-hewn roof timber (vigas) that extended playfully out through the tops of the exterior walls. And like many casitas in that area, it had floors made of lacquered tile and brick, and an adobe wood-burning kiva fireplace that just begged to be lit every night, even in the summer. I could deeply *feel* the decades of simple tradition-aware life that had been enjoyed there. There really was magic in this place—so I was eager to see if it extended to my writing.

It was early September, and the outside daytime temperature was a perfect 75°—typical for Santa Fe at that time of year. At a 7000-foot elevation, Santa Fe avoids the sweltering summer heat that bakes much of the desert Southwest. So on a table in Lance's backyard, surrounded by cottonwoods and adjoining adobe, I quickly set up my laptop and settled into the pleasant atmosphere of Northern New Mexico. And I started writing.

I started a bit hesitantly. But within a few minutes the words started to flow, and then they flowed some more. And within fifteen minutes they were rushing as fast as I could type. I couldn't *stop* writing! By the end of the day, the essence of my new book was taking form. I came back the next day, and by its end, Chapter 1 of the book you have in your hands had poured out almost in its entirety. The muses were at work.

And that was good because I really *had* been stuck on this book for many, many months. Earlier in the year, I had come to know that I needed to write a book about awakening. I needed to describe these experiences I was having—I needed to *share* this. You'd think that wouldn't be such a hard book to write: I should just sit down and describe what happened. But I'd been resisting writing about *myself*. I felt that writing in first person about awakening would be too presumptuous, as if I were bragging. And it could be a little too risky *professionally*. I don't usually write about spiritual topics, and my readers don't expect that. So I had been a bit torn with how, or even whether, to write the book.

But sitting there in the backyard of that Santa Fe adobe casita, what I needed to write came pouring out. There was something about the setting and the vibe of the surroundings that inspired me to throw caution to the wind and to write about *me* and *my* experiences. And there really was something about the muses of the area that caused the book just to *flow*.

In fact, I was so inspired by that outcome and the creativity of that setting that the next day, I rented an apartment there in Santa Fe, and over the following months and year, I traveled there for several weeks at a time. In doing that, I fell in love with the beautiful little city of Santa Fe, and I successfully completed this book you're now reading.

SILENCE AS THE STARTING POINT

But I'm getting way ahead of myself because while Santa Fe *is* a key part of this story, as you'll see throughout the book, the *beginning* of the story of awakening wasn't there in Santa Fe at all. It actually started two years earlier, at the end of 2012.

I was in a pleasant home in Alamo, California, a nice bedroom community near San Francisco. I had grown up in Alamo since age one, but our family left when I was ten and I didn't return until years later. It's an attractive valley town with oak tree–lined streets surrounded by steep parklike wooded hills, some of which even have formal wilderness status. The town is dotted with restored California ranch-style homes. In fact, Alamo started as a small ranching town in the late 1800s. Now it was a home for those seeking a peaceful repose from the busy San Francisco metropolis, twenty-eight miles away. My girlfriend of two years also lived here in 2012, and I was at her home for Thanksgiving dinner that year. It was at that dinner that I first noticed the experiences that later blossomed into a full-blown awakening.

Here's what happened. We had a group of friends over for the meal. I had cooked and carved the turkey, and we were all seated at the table with the meal spread out before us. Someone suggested that we take a moment of silent grace, and I closed my eyes with inward attention to do that. It turns out this was the first time in many years that I had closed my eyes with inner alert attention. Decades earlier I'd done it often—I used to meditate regularly. But that was a long time ago, and for some reason, this grace was my first resumption of any sort of meditative-like reflection. And as soon as my eyes closed, to my surprise pure silence came pouring in, in a very profound and delightful way.

To describe what that silence was like, I have this analogy: It's as if I'm floating in the middle of a perfectly calm lake on a dark moonless night. No wind, no sounds, nothing to see other than perhaps the indirect glow of the stars above. I'm intensely aware of the expanse of the still lake going on forever in all directions in that vast emptiness and silence. It's peaceful and I'm very alert and aware. I have a sense of awe in the freedom of my awareness, which is now not attached to any details, but is now free from worry or pursuits of life. I'm just sitting in that wide, infinite space.

That's the kind of silence and stillness I experienced back then and do now, often, when I take an inner silence session. I experience a vast shimmering alert silent space within which I sit.

In the days after that occurrence, back at home, I couldn't wait to repeat this. So I sat with my eyes closed, inwardly alert, a couple of times each day—and the silence came again and again, growing greater and greater. And except for some early "off" periods, it hasn't stopped since.

This first experience of deep profound inner silence is really only the beginning of the story, but it's an important beginning. That's because, as you'll see, inner silence is a fundamental and incredibly important component of awakening. And I'm not the only one who has found silence to be the basis of awakening. A similar description of silence is referred to over and over again in most other books and teachings about awakening, and in many different ways. Sometimes it's called stillness, sometimes pure awareness, and sometimes emptiness. No matter what you call it, it's the *foundation* of what I'm calling simple awakening.

WHAT KIND OF AWAKENING?

What a word, *awakening!* It can conjure up so many impressions. Awakening can be a risky word to use since it often elicits images that range from New Age zealotry to religious fundamentalism. So I tread carefully when I use it. But it's the *best* word to use because it accurately describes what's happening.

If you look up the word *awakening* in the dictionary, you'll find that it has a lot of definitions. However, I have a very specific definition in mind for it in this book, and in case you haven't yet figured it out, I'm talking about *awakening of consciousness.* It's sometimes called enlightenment, or liberation, or Self-realization. Buddhists call it *bodhi* or *kensho,* and sometimes *nirvana;* Sufis call it *al-insanul-kamil*; Hindus call it *moksha.* But the English translations almost always end up with *awakening.*

There are of course stages and degrees of awakening, and you'll see the one I'm going to describe is probably an early stage, though still very significant.

Before proceeding, however, I should mention that *other* definitions of awakening are usually highlighted in most dictionaries and academic writings. You'll see dictionaries often refer to awakening as intellectual inquiries of a philosophical nature, and I'm not referring to that definition because what I'm talking about is *experiential*—it's not a thought exercise. Also highlighted are historical trends of religion (e.g., the Great Awakening) and a number of specific religious movement that have the Awakening name.

Awakening of consciousness, or spiritual awakening, is much more fundamental, however, and much more important than any of these academic definitions.

If I had to give a one-sentence definition, I would define awakening as *expanding your consciousness to connect yourself with who you really are*. Beyond all the benefits I described in Chapter 1, that's really what I feel is going on with me right now. My conscious experience of life is changing, expanding, and I feel as if it's revealing the spiritual core of who I really am—with a ton of associated benefits.

However, that's an ambitious and perhaps even *vague* definition, and so it demands explanation. It's also a definition that could be applied to a number of more mundane growth experiences, ones that really are not spiritual in nature. So I'm going to sort this out initially by relating it to classical explanations of awakening of consciousness. Those reference points I'm comparing to are the written and recorded works of modern-day mystics, philosophers, physicists, and awakened teachers. I accept them and share them here because they match with my own experience and help explain it.

Not Religious

Notice that I'm mostly avoiding religious explanations in this book. That's because I can't call my current experiences religious—I'm not having experiences of a God form or contacting spirits, prophets, or the like. But that said, what I'm talking about can still be called *spiritual* in nature because there are significant spiritual implications to awakening of consciousness, even in these early stages. I think it's fair to say that the end of suffering is a spiritual experience, as is coming to sense the fundamental philosophical nature of life. Seeing a growing unity in all things in life is a spiritual experience as well.

There are many more advanced awakened individuals who say that some form of contact with God *is* the eventual outcome of growing awakening, and I look forward to that if so. At my relatively early stages of awakening, I can see how things are trending in that direction, which is gratifying. But in a way I'm glad I'm not having those experiences. How would I explain *that* to my colleagues!

Even without focusing on the more spiritual aspects, however, awakening is obviously still a very big deal. Everything I describe in Chapter 1 is happening now, and that list represents a profound and deep reorganization of my life. And as I said, it all begins with the experience of profound silence.

GROWING SILENCE

What is that silence? I'll get into that more ahead, but in brief, I understand it to be my direct experience of pure consciousness emerging and standing alone, unattached to objects of perception. Of course, what I just stated is a pretty heady definition, so let me continue to focus on my direct experience and what it meant to me.

After that first interesting experience at the holiday meal three years ago, the appearance of silence started to happen more and more often when I closed my eyes. After many such repetitions, I thought, *Hmm, something is happening here.* It felt good and profound, so I started taking regularly scheduled silent periods again, basically meditation, and sure enough, that silence became a common experience in those periods. Not the *whole* time and not in *every* sitting, but for significant portions of most sittings. Even if my mind became nearly full of thoughts, I was aware at most times that the silence was there beneath them, like a flat and vast infinite landscape plane (the silence) sitting under passing puffy clouds (my thoughts).

From that Thanksgiving of 2012, the silence continued to grow in my eyes-closed sessions. But then in 2013, I also started to notice that the experience of silence was existing *outside* of my eyes-closed sessions, in my activity. What I mean by that is that I could sense its presence along with my other perceptions. At times it was there just a little, but over time, it became quite a lot. As the months progressed, I found the silence was nearly always there supporting my thoughts, my actions, and nearly all my outer experiences. It seemed that my awareness was half on my current focus at the moment and half on the silent field that was underlying everything.

BENEFITS OF SILENCE IN EARLY STAGES OF AWAKENING

Before I explain more what that silence is, let me tell you what portions of the benefits I listed in Chapter 1 came at this early stage, so you know what to expect if you're trending in this direction.

First, the bliss was not there yet—that came later, as I'll describe in the next chapter. But nearly everything else I listed in Chapter 1 was showing up to *some* degree. I was getting happier; I was feeling a sense of growing meaning to life; life was getting easier with even more accomplishments and less striving; life was getting simpler, and things I needed were appearing more easily; the common little fears and concerns of life were diminishing; and intuition was growing. So a pretty good list of benefits was emerging! At the beginning of 2013, I saw only a little of each of these, but they grew month by month.

I didn't always directly relate things like this to the growing silence—how could I? Couldn't they be coming for other reasons? But there were many times, when silence in activity set in for an hour or so, that I *did* directly correlate them—many of them clearly occurred because the silence was there. Later, as the silence became a nearly full-time presence, the correlation for the whole package became undeniable.

There were also some interesting side effects as that silence came in. For example, when the silence came in strongly, I'd often feel a distinct energy or sensation in some different parts of my body that are classically associated with spiritual development. The brow area of my forehead (centered above my eyes) would become quite activated and energized when the silence was strong. It was as if all my attention and knowing were flowing through that area energetically. It was not unpleasant, but there'd be a noticeable intensity about it. I'd also often feel strong energy rising from the base of my spine and sometimes from elsewhere in my body. It's interesting that as I read the writings of others experiencing awakening, I see these are pretty common experiences.

WHAT IS SILENCE?

All right, let's discuss this silence more because at first this experience of silence can be confusing. This is one reason I'm writing this book—to discuss what silence is in a very practical way. It's possible that many people from all walks of life could be having some experience of growing silence, but they need advice on what it is. Some may not even realize how good a thing growing silence is since it feels so outside the norm. So what is this silence?

As I stated above, from all my reading, the best official definition I have is that my silent awareness is the direct experience of pure consciousness emerging and standing alone, unattached to objects of perception and growing in its own strength. That's what the silence is.

Here's how that silence *feels* to me. Intuitively, it feels as if it's the center of my being. It feels as if it's the source of the finer and nobler aspects of me. It feels like that which would be left if all *outer* aspects of life were gone—it's the core of who I am. In fact, it even feels as if it's the core of nature itself. These days, as I look around me, it's as if I can see that same silence in everything else, at least to some degree.

But that's about all I can say, experientially, without reaching for outside sources, without getting more guidance from classical writings on awakening and from teachers in the know. And so I have studied this extensively over the years since it started, and here are my insights.

One possible and very simple explanation of the silence is that I'm reaching a very profound relaxed physical state—one that is so distinctive and so absolutely still that it triggers rarely accessed capabilities of the human physiology. That explanation may be true—a lot of the benefits may be coming from a deep physiological rest I'm creating in my silence sessions.

However, I think the real answer is much deeper than that. In fact, with both my readings about awakening and observing how the silence works in me, I now know it's really a *lot* deeper than that.

A FIELD OF INFINITE POTENTIALITY?

To describe what I think this silence really is, let me get a bit philosophical and scientific. If this feels dry to you, bear with me—it's useful.

At the core of nearly all religions, and at the core of most philosophies, is the belief that there's an absolute presence or field that underlies everything, a source from which, ultimately, everything springs. This belief is most obvious in the Eastern religions and philosophies. But even in Western ones, if you dig into their more mystical sources, you'll find that same premise. You might say that this underlying field is the root energy that exists below everything. However, the word *energy* is wrong because that implies a level of expression or manifestation that isn't accurate. Rather, the field really is a *potential* to create all the energy and substance that we see around us and that exists in this universe. It's a field of infinite potentiality underlying, supporting, and even *creating* everything, moment to moment.

There have been a lot of books in the last few decades that say quantum physics points to such a root field of physical existence as well. This postulated field is called by various names, but the most common is *the unified field*. Some physicists say that this theorized but yet-to-be-proven field has a base, unmanifested state from which *all* reality emerges (and that it's analogous to the zero-point or vacuum state of electromagnetism—something that *has* been proven to exist).

A number of physicists (some of them quite well known) and nearly all philosophers who discuss this underlying field have postulated that this field is essentially *consciousness*. Many claim that humans, if they develop their consciousness enough, can experience and work from that root field of all reality. Many writers on the topic say this field is experienced as profound silence, stillness, or even *emptiness* (a term that writers on Zen often use). Essentially they are saying that a human's experience of profound silence is the same unmanifest field of infinite potential that physicists, philosophers, and even saints have been pointing to as underlying all of life, all of reality.

Nearly any book on Zen or spiritual awakening will lead you to this conclusion. If you want to study the postulated linkages between consciousness and *physics*, you might read the early classic books on the topic like *The Dancing Wuli Masters* or *The Tao of Physics*. A newer book on the topic is *The Self-Aware Universe*. Another newer but less technical book on the topic by a well-regarded astrophysicist is one called *The God Theory*. There are many more. All of these books postulate that consciousness is primary in the universe, and that all of reality springs from consciousness.

Now, try as they might, there's no way physicists or philosophers can prove all that. Math, measurements, and logic—they all give out before the connection between the postulated unified field of physics and the human experience of pure consciousness can be firmly established. As a result, the majority of *lay* physicists reject this notion as New Age musing. But judging from the immense amount of passionate writing on this topic, this correlation feels right to an awful lot of people. It certainly feels right to most current writers on spiritual awakening. And these days, it feels right to *me*.

Of course I too cannot prove that's what's happening in me or in others who are experiencing some form of awakening—and I don't even want to try. Rather, I'm happy to simply use it as a viable model or theory that both *matches* with my experiences and helps explain the *magic* of my experiences. It helps explain why they are so amazing.

For example, it explains why the silence I experience feels as if it's the core of who I am and everything else. After all, if ultimately all of us have sprung from that field of potentiality that physicists and philosophers talk about, then it should be at *my* core as well as all others'.

It also explains why I feel *supported* by the silence. After all, if it's my absolute core, then it will feel as if I'm coming home and it *will* support me.

It also explains why the experience feels so still and unwavering—the zero-point field of life *should* feel that way because by its very definition, it's the state where the outer vibrating form of reality nearly ceases movement.

It also explains why it feels as if the silence is bubbling with potentiality and even *wisdom*. That makes sense because if I can truly experience directly the root field of reality, I should also be able to access it as it just starts to manifest or unfold—in its about-to-express state. And that experience should be one of abundant potential energy and information.

It goes on and on. Again, at this point it's just a theory for me. But it and the theories of Eastern and Western mystics all combine into a cosmology that explains why my experience of silence is so profound, and so I choose to believe it. And I hope it helps explain to *you* why silence, even in the very first stages of awakening, is so important. It *is* desirable for you to start allowing silence to consciously establish itself in your awareness, so you can be supported by it.

In the end, though, it really doesn't matter if you believe this theory or not, because the results are the same. Once silence starts to move in, all the benefits I described happen nonetheless—no belief is required. Don't just take my word for that. There are a lot of Western writers who have also experienced this awakening and described it in the same ways—people like Eckhart Tolle, David Hawkins, Byron Katie, Anthony De Mello, Steven Gray (Adyashanti), and many more. I list these particular people because they are all English-speaking Westerners, often originally from nonspiritual backgrounds, who discuss their surprising experiences of awakening.

All of these people have descriptions in their works that match well with what I described above. And when they wax philosophical about where their experiences come from, they usually end up with a similar explanation to the theories above. That provides at least a little confirmation that the package of experiences called awakening is real, has profound philosophical explanations, and is experienced similarly for all those that have witnessed silence moving in like this.

PURE AWARENESS, PURE CONSCIOUSNESS

So far, over and over again I've emphasized the term *silence*. However, if you've read many other books on awakening, you may see other terms in addition to or instead of silence used to describe what their authors are experiencing. I use the term *silence* so much because that's the best way to describe the experience I had at the initial stages, when I first encountered this in my meditations: it was the quieting of thoughts and mental activity. And it wasn't just *verbal* thoughts that quieted down, it was also mental images, emotions, and sensory experiences; all of that settled way down when I sat in my silent sessions, often to a perfect calming of mental activity: just pure alertness.

You could also call the experience *stillness*, which many authors do. Eckhart Tolle often calls it *spaciousness* because that's one way to describe your sense of reality when your awareness settles down and spreads out. Some people call it *wholeness,* as that's often how it feels in its infinite connectedness. The term *pure being* is also used. Another term is *source*, and I'll use that term a lot in some contexts ahead. The Transcendental Meditation movement calls it *transcendental consciousness* or just *transcendence*. Another term a lot of others use is *Self* with a capital S (I'll talk more about using that term in the next chapter). You'll see all these terms used, and if you explore what's behind each of them, you'll see they generally mean the same thing.

Yet another set of terms to use for the pure silence I speak of is *pure awareness* and *pure consciousness*. From my readings on awakening, and from my later experiences, these two terms are probably the most *accurate* ones for describing what's going on when experiencing silence. That's because, at root, pure silence is really pure human awareness, pure consciousness, emerging from its hiding place so you can experience it directly. But I need to explain what I mean by that.

When silence comes in during my eyes-closed sessions, what I experience is being alert and very awake, but there's nothing, really, that I'm aware of. It is awareness by itself, in a pure and unattached form. That experience of being alert and awake by itself is a very big deal, because it represents the aliveness of who I really am, standing alone and clearly identifiable. It's the spark of life—the essence of my being. The old saying "I think, therefore I am" is wrong. The saying should be "I am *aware*, therefore I am." What's left when all else settles down is your ability to be aware. And while at first that is merely experienced as a lack of perception of other things—a silence—after a while, you experience that pure awareness as a strong *presence*, even in the midst of activity. So this is what silence is: it's pure awareness, pure consciousness, and it can grow to be a strong force in your life. Since it's the root of who you are and presumably the root of everything else, having that presence actively in your life is a very good thing.

In Closing: The Experience of Silence

While the terms I used above—pure consciousness and pure awareness—are probably the most *accurate* terms to describe silence, I don't like using these terms too much, particularly in beginning discussions. That's because at the early stages of awakening, they're mostly theoretical, so it takes thought to understand why those terms are correct. Discussing these terms usually brings one into his intellect, which leads away from direct experience. I'd rather focus on what I can say I *experience*, so that readers can relate it to their own experiences. In fact, much of this chapter has gotten a bit theoretical, which can be unfortunate when talking about the growth of awakening.

So to close this chapter, let me reemphasize what my inner experiences were like at the early stages, at the onset of simple awakening. I can say I experienced deep *silence* oftentimes when closing my eyes and staying alert, and that silence was very real to me. The silence felt profound and meaningful, and it felt like the essence of me. That same silence later moved into my activity, where it was also very tangible. It was as tangible to me as the air I breathe and the sunlight that filters through the sky, and it was just as beneficial. The correlation of silence with the beginnings of the benefits I listed in Chapter 1 was, even at the early stages, undeniable to me as a deep stability and happiness grew in my life. This is what I suspect you'll first experience, too, as you start experiencing early stages of awakening.

3.

THE IMMENSE FREEDOM OF AWAKENING

There was much more to come. That's because later a third stage of awakening was to arrive—something I call *true awakening*. It brought with it an immense *freedom* that is, perhaps, the most important aspect of simple awakening.

In the late spring of 2015, after about six months of flying back and forth between California and Santa Fe, I decided to stay permanently in my new writing home. Not only was Santa Fe friendly to my writing, but it was inviting to my soul. Underneath the adobe and charm of Santa Fe, there was a great depth that was resonating with me. My connection and familiarity with that depth became more and more important—to the point where I couldn't stay away. In a way, my growing bond with the state of New Mexico was paralleling my growing state of consciousness. It was as if the two "states" were inextricably linked.

I was sad to leave California; it ended my fifteen-year love affair with that state. That affair started way back in 1998, when I began living there for a second time. I was born and raised in the state, but my family left when I was ten. Many times I'd wanted to move back, but because it's an expensive state to live in, to truly enjoy California it greatly helps to have a lot of money. From my early careers, and after my first divorce on the East coast, I had not saved enough to buy a nice home in

California. But the opportunity to move there in style came in 1998 when I accepted a position at the Northern California offices of the large management consulting firm Accenture. It was a fast-track job with partner potential and a lot of excitement. Accenture gave me both a generous signing bonus and a generous moving budget, and those were enough to enable me to move from Washington D.C. into a nice section of Northern California, and to afford the down payment on an attractive home.

At Accenture in California, I was immediately making good money, and I was learning the business world inside and out. I moved into a senior position in their consulting line, helping some of the largest companies in the world create technology strategies and solutions to meet their business goals. Then I co-managed Accenture's Internet Centers of Excellence and helped our clients transition to Internet-based business. Next, for two years I was working onsite at eBay in a joint venture with Accenture, leading the technology portion of that venture. Later, after I left Accenture, I went on to write books and then create and present an advanced methodology about workday efficiency. Throughout all that time, I was very busy and I felt very important. This was the most dynamic stage of my life's career—and I was eating it up. And I was using my high income to greatly enjoy the beautiful state of California.

My whole time there I truly was living the California dream. The home I bought was on a lovely golf course a short drive from some of the best scenery California has to offer. Several times a month in my new BMW convertible, I'd take the most amazing top-down Pacific Highway drives. I'd usually drive either north up the Sonoma coast toward Mendocino or south through Monterey, Carmel, and down along the glorious Big Sur coastline. Napa was only an hour away from my home, and I'd take frequent back-road drives through the vineyards with my wife, tasting new wines and checking out new foods. I also loved hiking through the tall redwoods, exploring the low rolling coastal mountains and view-ing the towering and massive Sierra Nevada mountains, including those around Lake Tahoe and Yosemite. I loved the richness of California, and I remember commenting to friends, "I cannot imagine living anywhere else; this truly is me!"

However, near the end of my fifteen years there, I came to realize that it *wasn't* me—at least not the *inner* me. I came to realize that I had been enamored and lulled by California's outer perfection, and as a result I was no longer probing my inner depths. Despite the image of Califor-nia as being a consciousness-raising state, most Californians really are very *superficial*—and I had completely joined them in that superficiality, fully abandoning my earlier inward meditation career. It was easy to soak in California's outer beauty and think that I had found everything—but I hadn't.

Perhaps as a blessing, toward the end of my stay there, the perfection of California started slipping for me and most other Californians. The water shortage, which had recently been turning the lush irrigated greens to brown, was just part of it. Really, *dissatisfaction* was the only thing truly growing in this paradise because many other edges were also fray-ing. Primarily, the economy was still weak and everyone seemed short on money. In a place where conspicuous consumption means almost every-thing, when money runs short, so does the meaning of life.

For me, it wasn't just the diminishing dream, but it was also that my second marriage had failed and my work was getting harder. But even more important, I was receiving inner messages saying it was time to reach more deeply into the core of who I was. I was sensing the need for something much more profound. Even if the perfection of California *had* been maintained for me, I could no longer see living out my life just *consuming* that state. And even though I was helping a lot of people with my books and training, I felt I needed to contribute to the world in an even more profound way than that.

So in 2012, as the inner silence started to roll in and as my subsequent awakening experiences grew, I sensed that my true self was finally emerging. And with it, perhaps coincidentally, the now inauthentic hold California had on me began slipping away. And apparently, New Mexico, a state that was nowhere on my mind at that time, was plotting its move into my soul.

STAGES OF AWAKENING

Clearly, our lives can have stages and phases where various locations hold sway for us, and we can often track our material and personal progress through the history of the places we live. In a similar way, the growth of awakening has stages and phases that highlight our *internal* progress in an even more significant way. As I look back over the recent years of my emerging simple awakening, there seem to have been three distinct stages to that emergence.

As I've said, the first stage was experiencing deep silence nearly every time I closed my eyes with alertness; that started in November of 2012 at that fateful Thanksgiving dinner in California.

The second was when that silence continued after my eyes-closed session right into the background of my active day; that rolled in gradually throughout 2013, near the end of my time in California. It brought clarity and insight to my day, and it greatly supported everything I did. I wrote about this in the previous chapter.

The third stage, the topic of *this* chapter, is what I call *true awakening*. That's when I began to identify silence as being *who I really am*. This most recent stage started for me at the beginning of 2014, and it has been by far the most significant. It correlated, by the way, with the very beginning of my slow move to the magical New Mexico.

Making the distinction of this third stage of awakening experience is important because this thing I call true awakening represents a major step forward compared to mere growing silence. It is, I think, what most wise people refer to when they refer to *enlightenment, liberation, Self-realization,* and so on.

But before discussing true awakening, I first want to clear up what I think is a common *misunderstanding* about the type of awakening commonly referred to as enlightenment. Many books and movies that portray enlightenment imply that it's something a person slips into suddenly and completely, all in one step. One minute the protagonist is a regular Joe or Josephine, and the next minute he or she is fully enlightened, perhaps even without warning.

That description may be true for a very small number of people who have become enlightened, but I think by far that for most people experiencing awakening, it's not accurate. Rather, for most people I think all the stages of awakening are a *gradual* process, a process that occurs over years and perhaps over a lifetime. I think most awakenings are experienced with peaks and valleys along the way, with a long-term general upward trend. And again, *gradually*. So no, for most people who experience this, they're not walking around living normal life and one day suddenly slip permanently into enlightenment.

That said, during that gradual growth, a person might cross a threshold and notice a really big change. The first experience of true awakening I'm about to relay to you was an example of that for me—it was a major step into a different level of awakening that seemed to come all at once. But it only came for me after years of growth preceding it. And after it came, it disappeared for a while and then gradually and less abruptly came back again. Finally, more recently, it seems to have arrived permanently.

THE TRUE AWAKENING EXPERIENCE

What is a true awakening experience? The best way to discuss it is to describe how I first experienced it in January of 2014. I'll never forget this event, and I still talk of it often. And while it had immense implications, to describe it is really quite simple, so here goes.

As a backdrop, for the initial years that I was experiencing silence, while that silence felt very intimate and core to who I am, it still was *separate* from the majority of my life and from who I thought I was. Rather, I still identified with my career, my past experiences, my relations, my actions, my hopes, my dreams, my pains, and my concerns. If someone asked me who I was, some combination of those is what I described.

But one day in January 2014, I was sitting in my California living room overlooking the greens of the golf course and taking one of my daily silence sessions. In the middle of that session, my sense of who I was suddenly shifted. I found that instead of that profound silence existing separately from me, I experienced directly that *I was that silence*. In other words, my core *identity* shifted from being the normal me—from being the sum of my thoughts, goals, actions, and my life in California— to me actually *being* the silence underneath all that.

It was a very distinct experience. Suddenly, my normal identity and all its swirling energy of concerns, doubts, prides, activities, and world focus collapsed into a small spinning ball of energy off to my side—it was now sitting *outside* of me. The *true* me sat in the infinite field of silence that was clearly separate from that churning ball. I *was* that silence. The normal me off to the side now looked small and silly by comparison. The *true* me was vast, infinite, and incredibly peaceful, unmoving, and whole.

That's really all there was to it; it was a very simple thing, and it lasted for only a few hours. Weeks later, I found it coming and going again. Eventually, I found it stabilizing over many months in a more integrated fashion, in which the silent identity merged with the worldly identity and the two became more as one.

But even though on that first day it came for only a short time, it had a *huge* impact at the moment it did. That's mainly because of the intense contrast of its first arrival—it was so different from anything I had experienced before. Later, I got more accustomed to it as it became a regular part of life and as it integrated into my outer activities. Also, the first experience was very impactful because, when my identity shifted like that, some major "realizations" flooded in that permanently changed the way I looked at everything. What realizations?

First, it verified what I alluded to at the end of the last chapter—that pure awareness, silence, is who we really are. That's an entirely different identity from before awakening, and the philosophical implications of that were striking.

But even more important and more immediately noticeable was that I realized who I *wasn't*. I realized that the ragged and rugged swirl of my engagement with life wasn't me at all. My worries, my hopes, my concerns, my goals, and how I expressed all those in my personality—they all were not really me. Rather, I saw that all the hustle and bustle of my engagement with life was *outside* and *separate* from me. That little ball of swirling energy off to the side that I used to call me, it was now almost insignificant and laughable by comparison to the real me: an immense and infinite wholeness of quiet and lively silence and stillness. This shift was not an intellectual or conceptual one, it was totally *experiential.* My point of identity moved. The perspective and position from which I viewed the world shifted; I was now viewing the world from *inside* that silence, from *being* that silence. That shift in identity is what I call *true* awakening—I've awakened to who I really am—I *am* that silence.

In true awakening I also found that I immediately stopped taking the old me so *personally*. Nearly all the features of the old me were still there and I still engaged in the world through them, but they became tiny and almost inconsequential in comparison to the profundity of my actually *being* that deep silence that underlies all of life. For example, the typically threatening nature of day-to-day issues and concerns that many of us have—concerns about things such as whether I would get the next business deal, be stuck in traffic for hours today, get what I currently want, have people like and appreciate me, be hurt by what's going wrong in politics this week, make progress at work today, save enough money for retirement, or find love—all those and similar concerns virtually *vanished*. They just seemed so tiny by comparison to that profound silence being who I was.

One classic way to describe this experience that I'm calling true awakening is to say that I shifted from identifying with my *small* self (or *personality* self—the churning ball now off to the side) to identifying with my *larger Self*. The small self gets its name from how small it seems when compared to living the majesty and infinite expanse of that deep and profound silence. When that shift happens, the silence is then typically called the larger Self (notice the capital S in this instance of the word Self). The often used term *Self-realization* gets its name from that shift of identification to the larger Self—you realize you are the larger Self, the field of infinite silence.

IMMENSE FREEDOM

Obviously, the onset of that state resulted in a big (and very pleasant) contrast with the old me. There are many extremely important outcomes, but if I could sum up the impacts of that experience with one word, it would be *freedom*. A deep, profound, and immense sense of freedom suddenly overcame me. The swirl of my small-self life goes on, but I'm not *bound* to it, *attached* to it, *distracted* by it, or *pulled down* by it. My primary experience now is being free from all that silliness and identifying instead with the very blissful, wise, simple, yet infinite state of silence.

That immeasurable sense of freedom is one source of the word *liberation*, which you see in many books about enlightenment—you are finally free! It is a major and hugely important shift. When you experience it, you immediately know that it's the most important state anyone can reach in life. Our inner knowledge that such a state might exist is what explains why millions of people follow various teachers and religions that claim to offer it—I think we all intuitively know it *is* possible, and perhaps even unconsciously, we all seek it.

I want to repeat my main point with all this: Having your identity completely shift such that you *are* that silence—this is what I define as the line between *growing* or *onset* awakening and the experience of *true* awakening (whether permanently or only for a moment). You could also call this experience, even if just temporary, an experience of *enlightenment*, and many do. And I think it's safe to say that someone who has this experience most or all the time could be called enlightened or truly awakened.

Notice what I'm not including in this definition: I'm not talking about seeing God or the spirit world or auras, or having superpowers. I'm not talking about psychic abilities, cosmic visions, or traveling through the universe. And that's why my emphasis is on the word *simple* in my book title, *Simple Awakening*. This really is a very simple experience. It's incredibly profound but still very simple; your point of identity simply switches from the small self to the large Self. Everything changes, of course, particularly in your approach to and appreciation of life. But in a way nothing changes; the 3-D world remains the same.

BENEFITS OF TRUE AWAKENING

Because it's so simple, it's very hard to put into words how this sense of freedom and liberation feels and how important it is. So let me also focus on some other benefits of true awakening that are, perhaps, a bit more down to earth and easier to hang your hat on.

First of all, all the things I listed in Chapter 1 start to peak with true awakening. Things like freedom from the little and big fears and concerns that haunt you through the day; the sense of meaning and purpose in life that you gain; the ease with which you start moving through life; the way all activities get dramatically easier—and finally, how intuition starts to guide you, accurately, nearly all of your day. (I talk about this last point fully in Chapter 6.)

Perhaps the main noticeable thing that arrives is the incredible sense of rock-solid confidence and stability that comes from it. Your constant search for ways to verify your self-worth is now over. Let me talk about this last point in more detail, because it's hugely important.

The absence of and search for self-worth is a core motivator for most people, usually in an unconscious way. Many of us are so accustomed to it as an all-time reality that we don't even notice that we're constantly engaged in a search for self-worth, or how that search defines the manner in which we move through life. That search leads to some good behaviors (self-improvement, business creativity, willingness to work hard, kindness, and so on). But it also leads to many bad behaviors (greed, fear, jealousy, winning at all costs, and so on).

Ultimately though, the constant need to prove yourself to yourself and to others is completely unnecessary once you awaken to who you really are; motivation then comes from a much higher level.

The reason that your constant search for self-worth ends with true awakening is that your identity is no longer rooted in the small self. You see, it's the nature of the small self to be consistently feeling a lack of self-worth, and for good reason: in essence, the small self is a completely artificial construct. Even though we spend decades building and honing our self-image, that self-image exists only as a mental concept, and so it's not really a *thing*. There's virtually no spiritual or essential value to it, and in our core, we realize its inherent weakness. It can be challenged easily—and lost easily.

Fear of that loss dominates much of our lives. Think of the supreme importance of "saving face" in many societies. Think of the ongoing efforts we take toward maintaining our pride. Lifetimes are spent building and maintaining it, relationships are made and lost over it, and wars are even fought over it.

COMPENSATING SMALL-SELF STRATEGIES

As a result of its fragile self-esteem, the small self, in the absence of awakening, is constantly trying to reinforce itself, to prop up its worthiness. One way it does that is by comparing itself to others and trying to find reasons that it's better than others. That gives us an illusion of validation, of being in the right. We try to pound that illusion of higher position into place through innumerable means: making more money than others, owning better or smarter things, getting more power, being more clever, trying to learn and know more, looking better, becoming acquainted with better people, and so on. Clearly, such compensation efforts are at the root of much of society's obsession for more and more material gain, far beyond what we need to survive or even thrive.

But the satisfaction from each gain in esteem only lasts a short while. That's because someone is always there who can outclass us in one or another measure. When we see that, almost immediately the weakness of the small self becomes blazingly obvious, and once again we struggle for more verification. While this may sound childish—and it is—the only real change in adulthood is that we become more sophisticated in how we do it, and we push much of it below the conscious level. Nonetheless, it guides us nearly all our lives.

Another way the small self tries to cope with its inherent weaknesses, particularly in adult life, is through using *logic* to explain why life doesn't work right or feel secure. We analyze the discomfort as a problem to be solved, and we veer off in an amazing array of directions in search of solutions. We might logically identify illnesses or personal faults that explain it and then implement complicated cures, detailed diets, exercise crazes, psychology solutions, or new technology trends, all trying to explain and solve our faltering sense of self-esteem.

At the level of entire societies, ideologies are created and promulgated that promise to cure society's disconnected feelings. Many of the political, social, and religious approaches to life that leaders create and masses of people follow are simply reactions to the ongoing sense of unease of the members' small selves. The various solutions never solve that core problem, but they can, to some degree, provide the illusion of explanation and so provide comfort. Often, those compensating worldviews are just a distraction. For example, the shallow ways we measure our teams and tribes socially against each other, while lamentable, usually do no significant harm.

However, in other forms, they can lead to large wastes of social resources; think of all the laws passed against victimless crimes and the money spent and lives lost enforcing them. Sometimes compensating social ideals are even used to discriminate against others or as ways to force a way of life onto others. Think of the tragedy of persecution and genocide. Think of the world's history of religious wars. There's a lot of ugliness in society that can be traced to our lives being run by our insecure small selves.

At the individual level, all that changes when your identity shifts to the larger Self, which is that infinite field of silence that underlies all things and that truly is you. When that happens, the constant insecurity felt from your small-self identity vanishes. All the constant struggles to prove yourself go away. The events of life are no longer tossing your sense of worth about like a leaf in the wind. Just think if that were also applied at the level of society.

RAGING RIVER ANALOGY

Let me describe how this profound stability feels with an image that came to my mind when I had my first experience of true awakening. This analogy describes well the before-and-after experience.

Imagine you're immersed and being swept along in a raging river without a boat, without a raft, without even a life vest. You can barely keep your head above water to breathe as you bounce around in the river's currents and eddies. The image of you in this river is a metaphor that represents you in your stream of life in this wild world, and your tenuous sense of stability within it.

You live your whole life in that river. In your younger years, you're constantly hitting rocks in the river, rocks that you don't see coming. As a result, you're constantly injuring yourself, and you're often thrashing about and terrified by the lack of control. That said, sometimes people are there to help you, or sometimes smooth sections of the river appear where you can float easily and enjoy the ride. The problem is you don't know when the river is going to change back into rapids again, which it often does. When it does, you're back to bouncing off rocks again.

With time you learn how to avoid many of the rocks. You memorize where they tend to be and how they look just under the surface. You also build up protection mechanisms so they don't hurt so much when they hit. But you continue to get hit because you just can't see many of them coming.

As you mature in your life in the river, you start to realize that if you grab onto large logs that you see floating by, you can add security to the rough parts of your trip. These logs—ones that often have others on-board—represent social structures, relationships, careers, and so on. They might be groups of people you live with or identify with, belief systems that give you some mental stability, or even possessions that feel significant. You grab onto these logs and hold on for months or years at a time because the stability they offer is sorely needed. As a result, they come to represent portions of your developing self-image.

But unfortunately, they're really not that solid, and periodically those logs get knocked out of your arms or even break apart completely as they hit big river rocks. When that happens, once again you're out thrashing about in the current, desperately looking for something else to hold on to. And even when you do find them, all the logs seem amazingly slippery, so you often cling desperately and frantically even when you do seem to have a good one. If other people float into your space and threaten your hold on your logs, you might even lash out at them in fear.

Then one day you have a realization. Instead of constantly looking over the horizontal surface of the water for better and sturdier things to latch on to, to support you, you decide to go deep. You reach down with your normally floating legs and you find a rock-solid river bottom to stand on. This river bottom exists everywhere, under the entire river. You find you can stand on it at any time and remove yourself from the thrashing current. What an amazing awakening to find that underlying stability!

The experience of true awakening of consciousness, of establishing your identity in pure silence, is like touching bottom in the river and finally standing tall and free. Suddenly the whole world stops spinning around you, and you can see it a hundred times more clearly. You are now connected to an infinitely solid and stable platform. You can now finally understand what's going on around you because you have a clearer and broader perspective as you stand and survey the stream of life. You see simply that you were caught in a swirl most of your life, but now that swirl is separate from you and not influencing you so much or at all. Your fears and concerns drop away, and your expectation of constantly changing uncertainty around you ceases. A supreme sense of rock-solid confidence sets in.

As a result, you can actually start to deeply enjoy all aspects of the river of life, because you can see it clearly and appreciate its foundations and subtlety, including aspects you never noticed before during your thrashing. You may even start to see beauty and magic in the river of life that you never were able to witness when the fear of being tossed about was a constant underlying thing. Welcome to true awakening!

IS THE SMALL SELF AN ILLUSION?

Earlier in this chapter, I described the small self as being tiny and almost insignificant when compared to the larger Self (pure silence). I also mention that the small self is, in essence, a mental concept, and that's why it's not very strong or stable. So the question arises, does that mean your small self, your unawakened identity, is an *illusion?* That's what some spiritual leaders and writers seem to say. In fact, some say *all* of our 3-D reality is an illusion and that you'll realize that with awakening. Is any or all of that true?

Well, no—at least not at my simple stage of awakening experiences. Perhaps with some later stage of full enlightenment, with a more elevated perspective, I'll see that is true. But at these beginning stages of true awakening, the small self and our 3-D reality are both quite real to me, and I suspect they will be to you. It's just that our *relationship* with them changes dramatically. As I described above, because in awakening you're rooted in the truth of silence, you don't take the small self and 3-D world so *personally*. They don't capture your being or your identity anymore.

But you *do* maintain a significant partnership with them, and your small self continues to be the major projection of who you are into the world. It represents your personality, and so it's your primary mode of interacting with the world. It just doesn't *own the game* anymore.

In a way, you could say it's only with true awakening that you start to get the most out of your small self, your personality self. That's because the small self then takes the role it should take, as a friendly intermediary between your inner larger Self and the outer world. The small self no longer has the responsibility of completely explaining the fundamental meaning of the world or your essential role in it—something it was never equipped to do. It no longer has to guide and support you through the perils of life—it never had a broad enough perspective for that. Those are things the larger Self excels at.

I found that, after regularly having and stabilizing the experience of true awakening, I literally made friends with my small self, my personality self, in a way I never had before. I gave it a break when it made mistakes; I even found myself sending it love during its foibles. A father-son relationship has formed, with the all-knowing and all-loving larger Self holding the fatherly role and the small self being like a delightful child who plays with the world.

So no, the small self is not an illusion. It's a very real and very useful part of your life. It just works infinitely better when it's supported by your larger Self.

THE BLISS OF BLISS

There's an interesting thing about the benefits I list above. As amazing as they all sound, including the sense of supreme stability I described above in the river analogy, after a while they settle in and you actually start to get accustomed to them. You can even stop noticing them, unless you seem to drop out of awakening for a while (a common experience in the early stages). Or perhaps you see or hear the dramas or insecurities in the life stories of others and you think, "Oh yeah, my life used to be like that."

But one of the added "features" of true awakening that I *never* really get used to—that I never stop noticing, especially when it's there strongly—is the *bliss* that I described in Chapter 1. It arrived at almost the same time as my first true awakening experience, and it's a lovely thing! I want to talk about that a bit since it's so important.

As I said in Chapter 1, the best way to describe this bliss is as a profound *sweetness* that starts in my gut and then saturates my entire body and being. Try to imagine the sweetness of honey spreading throughout your whole self, and that will get moderately close to what it's like. Another way to describe it is this: imagine the satisfaction of eating the most delicious food; combine that with the most lovely physical aspect of making love; combine that with the warmest unconditional love you feel for your spouse and children; and merge in the most sublime feeling you have when in the beauty of nature—mix all those together and multiply them a few times, and that is what I call bliss.

Bliss is rooted in silence—it comes from silence, from pure awareness. And apparently the deep realization that silence is who I am (true awakening) is what triggers it.

Bliss can be experienced as a physical feeling, but it goes well beyond that because it penetrates *everything*, including my emotions, my thoughts, and my very being—it's hard to be captured by smallness, anger, sadness, or *any* negative emotion when bliss is present. Even the outer world seems to glow from the inner presence of bliss.

Here are some more details of my experience. In the beginning days of January 2014, the more noticeable aspects of bliss almost always started in my morning session of silence. There was an afterglow after that morning session—even though the bliss actually left afterward, my day still felt transformed. It was as if the echoes of that sweetness lingered into the day.

Also in the early months, there were just as many days when the bliss and the silence never came at all—even weeks of that. And in those periods, it felt as if I had crashed back down to earth since the contrast of returning to normal life was so great. If those periods were long, I'd start to get caught up in life's smallness and concerns again. I'd revert to my old coping mechanisms of looking for reasons for the moment-to-moment problems in life, trying to fix them and seeking happiness beyond them in the *things* of life that I thought I wanted and that I would try to chase down. Those approaches appear to work in their context, but they're just so small compared to awakening experiences, in which perceived problems go away spontaneously in a life generally guided by intuition.

Luckily, for me those off periods at first lasted only a few months, then only a few weeks, and then only a few days at a time. And as of this writing, periodic returns to my original unawakened and normal state seem to have completely ceased. Rather, identity with silence and the corresponding bliss are now present to some degree nearly all the time, either in the background or prominently up front.

Bliss has a wonderful effect on enjoying life, whether I'm alone or with friends, and whether I'm working or playing. It accentuates everything in life. Bliss also seems to add wisdom to life. While it's at the forefront, the underlying simplicity of how life works and how it is self-supporting, becomes my dominant awareness.

Now, I've just said that bliss accentuates life and wisdom. Actually, it's more accurate to say it the other way around. Being identified with the core of life, which I now know is that *silence* that is me, leads to bliss. In fact, I think bliss is just the outer expression of being one with that silence. Ultimately, all the benefits of bliss are brought on by *identifying* with silence. Bliss, I think, is a primary way that identity with silence is *expressed.*

THE WHY OF BLISS

But that leads to an interesting question: How can bliss be explained by the theory of silence that I covered in Chapter 2? The physics-based explanations I relayed there are intriguing, but why should an underlying field of potentiality be experienced as *bliss*?

Well, I don't think physics *can* explain it—that explanation can take you only so far when discussing awakening. One *philosophical* backing comes from the Vedas of India. Those ancient texts state that the field of infinite potentiality I've been talking about in this book is called *pure Being*, and that pure Being, when experienced, is experienced as bliss—as a feeling of supreme satisfaction, ecstasy, and exultation. Other philosophies say pure Being is experienced as pure *love.* And pure love, by the way, is not a bad description of the bliss I experience.

My intuitive theory of why that experience of bliss is occurring, a theory that dovetails with all these explanations, is this: Bliss is the natural reaction of human physiology to bringing that field of infinite potentiality fully into conscious awareness. Think about it. If during true awakening you experience the freedom I described above, then the exhilaration of that freedom might be experienced as extreme joy or bliss.

And finally, one last theory. Perhaps our human physiology is genetically designed to encourage connecting to infinite potential, to pure silence, because it's such a *beneficial* connection. Perhaps bliss is a DNA-programmed reaction. After all, procreation of our species is equally important, and the human physiology encourages it in a somewhat similar way, doesn't it?

No matter what the reason for bliss, it's a wonderful aspect of true awakening that I never get used to.

WHY IT'S CALLED "AWAKENING"

Why is the experience I'm describing in this chapter called "awakening"? Well, for good reason.

Remember the last time you awoke from a dream-filled sleep? Prior to waking up, while in the dreaming sleep, you were living various scenes of dream life in an active and seemingly real world. For most of us, we are completely immersed in our mid-sleep dream while it's going on, thinking that it's our reality. Bits of logic may slip in and tell us that it doesn't make sense, but generally we exist as ourselves when dreaming in sleep. In other words, we *identify* with the self that is in the dream.

Then when we wake up from the dream, our first thought is "Oh, that was just a dream." We immediately realize that the reality we were living in is not our true reality, even though just a moment ago we thought it was. We remove our self-identification from the "me" that was living the dream and move it to the me who lives our normal waking state.

That same degree of contrast is what you'll experience when your identity shifts from the small self to the larger Self, to that silent stillness that is truly you. You awaken to your real Self. By comparison, your small self now seems trivial! To think that you were identifying with the swirl of life's concerns, issues, limitations, and so on—it becomes abruptly apparent that it's not really you, and that you're way above that. It really is like awakening from a dream—a dream that now seems unreal in comparison to the new reality. And so that's why it's called awakening. It's as profound a shift in consciousness as moving from dream sleep to ordinary life, but even more so.

Another reason to call it "awakening" is due to what I alluded to in the last chapter. I stated that silence is actually pure *awareness*. As pure awareness grows, it's experienced as a growth of inner wakefulness, inner alertness; a silent witness becomes predominant behind all that you do. In fact, in the Transcendental Meditation movement, the first stage of enlightenment is identified when that witnessing element becomes so strong that awareness is present even in deep sleep. So what better term to use for the moment profound alertness or wakefulness becomes a full-time reality: awakening!

SIMPLICITY

The things I described immediately above—silence being pure awareness, and how awakening can be identified as when that witnessing element dominates in life—can sound a bit complicated. That wording is rather abstract and theoretical. So I want to step back a little and emphasize that true awakening, at least at the stage I'm experiencing it, is also a profoundly *simple* experience. After the contrast has worn off, you'll likely find that the experience of *being silence* is actually a very nondescript thing. In fact, many Buddhists call that experience "emptiness," and in some ways that's not a bad description.

You see, you might say that awakening is a *removal*—it's a removal of your (essentially mistaken) identification with the innumerable smaller details of life. When you step away from that identification, you suddenly see that your old identification with the small self was a very *complex* one. It takes a lot of energy and attention to try to track and control all of the intricacies of life lived as the small self. It takes great effort to monitor and solve the many problems of life when you approach them on the same level of the problems. In that complexity and effort, your identity becomes defined by reacting to and hopefully solving the challenges of life. Or even being defeated by many of them. That big, complex, collection of experiences becomes who you are.

With true awakening, as the major problems of life move to the side, you immediately see that the old identification as a problem experiencer and solver is *inaccurate*—it's not who you really are—and you can relax. You don't have to try to track and control life anymore because life becomes simple and easy. Life becomes spontaneously guided day by day, and moment by moment, by silence (as expressed primarily through your intuition, which I discuss in Chapter 6). You're off the hook to explain and solve all the complexities of unawakened life.

When that misidentification with the many details of managing life is released, what's uncovered then is supremely simple: You are that very simple and often blissful silence, the stillness that is the essence of life. You can't and don't want to try to track it. You can't and don't want to *control* the essence of life. You can only *be* it, and that act of *being* is a very simple thing. Everything emerges from it in very simple ways.

After a while, you start to realize that living life is no big deal— you just *are* that and you live your life almost automatically. The huge fuss most people make about the successes and failures of life then seems almost weird by comparison. Why make such a fuss when life is so simple?

Let me reemphasize one point about this simplicity. Notice that as I describe my experience, I'm not saying that with true awakening one starts living in other dimensions or that one gains superpowers. Things like that are sometimes associated with the terms *awakening* and *enlightenment*. I remember my first readings about awakening many decades ago in the book *Autobiography of a Yogi*. In that book the author described enlightened Masters he encountered in India who clearly did have superpowers. They could heal others, they could change the internal experience of others with a tap of their hand, and they could travel into other dimensions and come back and describe those cosmic worlds. But that's definitely not *my* experience.

My experience is so much simpler than that. While a deep freedom and richness has been added to my life with many very pleasant periods of bliss, those otherwise flashy things I read in that book and others have not come to me. I believe at a point in one's growth, some, or all of that, *could* also happen—possibly. I suspect things like that may be associated with *full* enlightenment—that rare state you read about in spiritual leaders once they reach the ultimate degree of awakening. Or perhaps certain pathways of awareness can be selectively opened for some people in earlier or later stages, and so they have experiences like that on and off.

But at this stage, to me the real nature of awakening, the *heart* of true awakening, lies in the simple *freedom* that comes when your identity shifts to who you really are: that pure silence, that stillness, that infinite potential that underlies life.

IN CLOSING

To close this chapter, let me reemphasize this: When the day-to-day fears and concerns of life disappear and a profound sense that all is well takes their place, life is lived in simplicity. It's not complicated, but it's very profound. And because it's so simple and natural, it is something I firmly believe many people can obtain. I truly believe that it's everyone's birthright—*your* birthright—should you choose to pursue it, should you choose to allow it in.

4.

How to Culture Silence for Awakening

As these experiences of simple awakening arrived for me and I saw the incredibly positive effect they had on daily work and life, I started to wonder how I could explain them or even teach them to others. As an author of books about making people's work and life more efficient and less stressful, I was dedicated to improving the lives of others. So it was no great leap to see that if I could help others achieve even a fraction of the simple awakening experience, doing so would accomplish far more for them than all my other efforts combined. Was there some way that I could teach this awakening to others?

Soon after coming to Santa Fe, in late 2014 and early 2015, I learned that one of the subcultures here was a diverse group of people who, starting in the sixties and seventies, came seeking spiritual insight. Back then, as now, many people were sensing the magic of the place and also responding to several famous writers who identified it as a consciousness-raising destination. Some of the organizations here today are the same groups that were teaching paths to awakening in the sixties and seventies.

If you grew up in those decades, you may know that all over the country, tens or perhaps hundreds of movements and techniques sprang up variously claiming to get you to higher states of consciousness.

Most of these teachings died out over time, probably because very few if any people succeeded with them. And many were pretty out-there groups, often guru-personality focused but lacking any genuine path to advancement.

However, some of those groups *were* good and effective, and as of today, a small number of them have survived—not only here in Santa Fe, but all around the country. And newer ones have popped up to join them.

POPULAR WAYS TO AWAKENING

The current count of groups focused on awakening that I hear about these days is small, though. When I look at *recent* media coverage of the consciousness-development genre, only a tiny handful of groups are talked about regularly these days. In fact, the only ones commonly mentioned are variants of Buddhism and a small number of similar Eastern tradition–based spiritual organizations that you can join. But are these options for you? Joining some of these organizations is almost like joining a religion and its community—you have to adopt a new belief system and a new way of life. Few of us want to do that.

There are also related movements still mentioned in the national media, like a few Mindfulness teachings and Transcendental Meditation (TM), that require no commitment to a spiritual belief system and that are more focused on *techniques*. Or you may see an offshoot Christian or Jewish or Muslim organization that offers deeper and more mystical spiritual instruction than you would normally see in the lay form of these religions that may also allow you to keep your root beliefs. One of these approaches might be more acceptable to you than others, and if you're using one of them successfully now to develop awakening, stay with it.

However, I meet a lot of people who say even these approaches don't feel right to them or haven't worked for them. For example, perhaps you've given up on anything that traditional religions have to offer as being too shallow and rule based. Similarly, with approaches that stem from ancient Eastern traditions, you may hesitate to jump into a system that was founded by a man with long hair or a shaved head, or from someone wearing white or orange robes. Or you might hesitate to adopt a system that tells followers to walk through life watching everything they do and think. Many approaches have sets of disciplines that seem too rigid, too extreme, or simply too unnatural for the average Westerner.

And yet, if you still want to learn more about and progress with awakening, what really are your choices?

By now you may realize that the awakening experience is not an East Indian experience, a Chinese mystical one, or a Christian one. Rather, it's an experience that is so naturally a part of everyone's human nature that it fits right in with everyday life—while taking life to an incredible new level. My point is, if it's as natural as I and others say it is, it seems as if there should be no need to sacrifice important aspects of your current life to reach awakening. It also seems logical that there should be no need to adopt serious disciplines or alternate mindsets that run counter to a comfortable Western lifestyle. It seems as if you should not need to become a monk and you should not need to pay rigorous attention to your thoughts. You shouldn't need to sit with a stiff posture. Really, you shouldn't need to do anything that is uncomfortable.

I have wrestled with those same issues and questions, and I've stayed completely with my Western lifestyle. I've only added a few things, and somewhat to my surprise, I've come out the other side successful, with a deep and profound growing awakening.

In fact, awakening snuck up me when I was doing *nothing* to attend to it. Rather, I was very busy with my business—awakening wasn't anywhere on my mind at the time. But it had been before, on and off quite extensively, and it has always remained a solid part of my belief system throughout my life. So was that part of the success?

Briefly, let me fill in some of the blanks in my story, and perhaps this will provide some context for your life with awakening.

MY EARLY ATTEMPTS AT AWAKENING

I started meditating in 1969, when I was fifteen years old. I had been looking for a meditation approach after reading some books on the topic that year. The meditation style I started then was the only one I could find: a Buddhist variant. While it was taught to me by a monk with a shaved head and long orange robes, thankfully he didn't require me to match that or join his group—he just taught me a mental technique to do every day on my own. But for some reason I didn't stick very long with the daily practice; I quit it after only a month.

The next time I tried meditation was two years later as a senior in high school. A friend there was practicing Transcendental Meditation (I'll abbreviate that as TM from here on) and he took me to a lecture. I signed up right away for the course, learned it quickly, and I stuck with it, doing it regularly, twice a day, through my college years and into my work and family career—a total of 35 years before I stopped. In the later portion of those years, I moved on to more advanced forms of the TM practice called the TM-Sidhis. Over the whole time, I saw a ton of benefits in my outer life, and I even had some early experiences of growing silence in my awareness that came but then went.

I stopped meditating around 2004. I was very busy with work and I was unhappy in life due to a failing marriage. Both those conditions distracted me greatly, and my meditation practice fell by the wayside. Luckily, though, after some years, I recovered a fairly happy and balanced work and social life again, and I considered starting meditating again. But just before I did, I had the experience I described in Chapter 2: suddenly and unexpectedly discovering silence moving into my awareness in a major way. It came on its own—I had done nothing to encourage it in the days, months, or many years immediately before that. I wasn't reading about awakening, and I wasn't practicing any form of meditation.

So the question is, did my earlier years of meditation practice set me up for this later growth? Or did just *living my life* lead to the growth toward awakening? Or was I perhaps cosmically scheduled in some way to start experiencing awakening at about that time?

I have no way of confidently answering those questions. I can say this: I never forgot about the possibility of awakening over those busy years while focused on work and life issues; I just put it by the wayside. And I firmly believe my previous decades of meditation established a degree of growth and momentum that never went away. Furthermore, I do believe that there was some *timing* involved, and my focus on life's trials was a part of that timing.

From my experience, there's no step-by-step process that I can point to that would allow me to say, "Do this and you will reach awakening." I do believe that all three elements I describe above contributed to my success. And if I were to suggest to someone who was seeking awakening how to pursue it, I would recommend the same three elements: having an interest in or awareness of the idea of awakening; taking inner silence regularly using a meditation-like technique; and being cognizant of life's timing. Let's go over each of these individually.

TAKING AN INTEREST IN AWAKENING

I firmly believe that if you wish to reach some level of awakening, you'll want to keep your awareness on that intention to some degree. You'll want to refresh the idea in your mind, even if it's only as a possibility and even if only for a little while each week. You want to keep the flame of your interest in awakening alive.

This is rather simple. It could mean periodically reading about awakening. Or it could mean occasionally thinking about what it is and how it can benefit your life. Or it may mean having a strong desire for it throughout your life.

There are many reasons why keeping at least some awareness on the idea of awakening helps *develop* awakening. First of all, I'm sure you've heard the expression "what you put your attention on grows in your life." That expression is true, and I believe it works with growth toward awakening as well.

But there's a larger reason here. While awakening is a very natural stage of a human's maturation, of a human's growth, it's not necessarily an *automatic* stage; some intention is usually required to initiate and maintain its growth. And as awakening arrives, it's important that you recognize what's going on and don't push it away. So it takes extra effort to seek out an awakening path and act on it even more consciously. Again, that means reading about awakening, putting your awareness on what awakening is and what it looks like, and setting a field of intention that awakening is really what you want next in life. This doesn't have to be arduous, just a choice to favor that study periodically.

For example, in my early and later stages of meditating, I made a point that about every third or fourth book I read was one about awakening or a related topic. My intention wasn't necessarily to follow any guidance in the books (there are so many different instructions out there, and many are contradictory), but rather just to keep the goal and description of awakening fresh in my mind. Reading books is just one example; listening to talks on the topic is another. Really, there are lots of ways you can keep the flame alive in your awareness.

All that said, I don't think you need to go overboard on this. You don't need to move in with a group of spiritually minded people. You don't need to avoid the non-spiritual aspects of everyday life. You don't need to make a religion out of it. Just keep the goal in the back of your mind and then live your life as you would otherwise live it.

As I look back on my life, that intention has always been there, either at the surface or just below it. Even when I completely stopped meditating and was focused strongly on my career (and an unhappy home life), there was always an inner knowing that there was much more to life than those things. Movies and fictional stories about regular people discovering they were much more than they thought they were consistently caught my eye. And from some inner hidden place, that knowing was always part of who I was.

TAKING REGULAR PERIODS OF SILENCE

Let's move on to the second element of developing awakening: taking frequent and regular periods of inner silence. This is an important element because it's a direct step in the direction of what you want: silence. From the previous chapters, you can see that internal silence is the hallmark of initial awakening. So it's obvious that taking time to culture that silence directly is time well invested. I feel anyone seeking awakening needs to do that. You need to take regular periods of inner silence so that the mind becomes familiar with the experience of silence and then starts to automatically invite it in. You want the mind to make a habit of noticing and accepting silence.

There are number of methods for taking silence, and most of them are a form of what you might call meditation. Nearly all organizations that teach awakening of consciousness teach some form of meditation or sitting in silence. And I firmly believe that nearly any of them can be used successfully, as long as they adhere to some basic principles that I believe are needed to be effective.

This is a long topic, and to give it the justice it deserves, I've devoted an entire chapter to it—the next one, Chapter 5. Feel free to either read that chapter *now*, or wait until after you finish this one.

Life-Cycle Timing

Finally, the third element in culturing awakening is to be cognizant of life-cycle timing. What I mean by that is being aware that there are biological and experiential cycles in your life that you lack control over and that you need to be at peace with. This is an important part of the lesson because you can take hours of silence every day and you can spend hours daily reading about awakening, but unless the life-cycle timing is right, neither onset awakening nor true awakening can come. Make peace with that and live your life accordingly.

Let's talk a bit more about this. I'm sure you know there are cycles to nature and life and some can be years or even decades in length. While some cycles are age-based and predictable (puberty for example), many cycles are much subtler and less understandable. Millions of people believe in the cycles of astrology, for example. Millions more simply witness the ebb and flow over time of health, prosperity, happiness, and so on, and they realize that the timing of events in life is more complex and more unfathomable than you or I could ever decipher.

The key is that such cycles can influence when and how we experience awakening. One person could begin taking silence sessions every day and within weeks start to have profound experiences of silence. Or a person could be like me, meditating twice a day every day for decades before detecting anything that I could call pure silence. Or like my more recent experiences, one could be in a period of focus on outer life instead of on awakening and find the greatest awakening results come then. There's no way to predict this and no way to control it.

My lesson to you is to be patient and to follow your intuition. There may be times in your life when the right thing to do is to focus primarily on your day-to-day work and family life, times when a focus on awakening is appropriate, and times to mix the two. Your intuition will tell you what's right and when it's right. If you're drawn to taking inner silence and it feels good to do it, and if it fits into your life, then do it. In contrast, if you were dragged to it, (say, by a partner) and you just don't like it, then don't do it. And there are other details that will vary from person to person, such as how long and how often to take silence. Guidance on all of this I feel can be accessible through your intuition, your gut knowing.

If you're thinking that you don't yet trust your intuition on matters like this, the good news is, once you start taking silence and developing awakening, it's likely that your intuition will grow to the point that you'll *know* what the right focus is at various stages of your life. I have a whole chapter on intuition ahead, but for now, know that this should not be a battle—simply find your inner knowing to whatever degree you can and follow it. If you do, awakening will come at just the right moment for you and with the least forced behavior. For some of you that may be many years down the road—so don't expect instant results from your silence sessions or from your other focuses on awakening. There will likely be many benefits well before then, though, so it won't be a hopeless wait.

LIVING YOUR LIFE

This brings up an important point. You need to live your life fully—don't drop out of life in the name of seeking awakening. This is something many young people did in the sixties and seventies and many regretted it later. Rather, embrace all aspects of life fully at every stage of your practice.

For example, you may be aware that there are monastic paths and non-monastic paths to awakening. Monastic paths require you to withdraw from normal life, usually to a monastery or ashram, often changing your dress, your diet, your surroundings, and even your family. This is an option for anyone, but it's probably not a comfortable or appropriate one for most Westerners. Imagine taking on an austere life, giving up progress with your career or family, but then not reaching any sort of awakening for decades—if at all. You might feel you wasted a life!

Unfortunately, though, many of the well-known current teachers of awakening grew up in a monastic lifestyle, and because of that, a monastic lifestyle often gets associated with awakening. For many of them, since life as a monk is all they know, they include monk-like principles when they teach their steps to awakening—it's part of their tradition of life.

Not only is that unfortunate, but I think it's completely unnecessary. I feel the appropriate awakening path for the cycle of life that most of us are in these days is a fully Western one. Most of my readers are living in an age of material gain and family life. You *can* succeed with awakening while living a life of normal activity; I certainly did. You do not need to withdraw from life to awaken.

That said, a small number of you may be in a life cycle where to withdraw into a monastic lifestyle feels like the right thing to do, and for a very few of you, it might in fact be right. But if you're feeling that way, and about to take that drastic plunge, make sure you're doing it for the right reasons.

For example, the awakening path should not be used as a diversion from an unhappy life. It should not be used as an alternate lifestyle to avoid facing the lessons of life head-on. I'm sure you've seen people who do this; people who use magical thinking about spirituality to avoid confronting life's issues. One common term for that is *spiritual bypass*. Please don't use the concept of awakening that way—don't use it as a Pollyannaish ideal to hold in your mind to try to explain away the roughness of life.

Certainly, the experience of awakening *is* magical, and it *does* transform your life in an amazingly profound and positive way. But those changes come on *top* of your normal life, not instead of them. Awakening for many is the endpoint of a long set of normal-life lessons that develop character and maturity along the way. In my mind, many of us must earn the right to awakening by living that maturation process.

AWAKENING IN THE LATER STAGES OF LIFE

In fact, I believe awakening may be easiest to achieve in the later stages of one's life, after living a full life. If you think of the stages of life from infancy to old age, I'd suggest that you can insert awakening as one such stage in the later parts of life. In many ancient cultures, it was assumed that at a certain older stage of life, a person would retire from his or her successful activity of making a living and raising a family and shift his attention to spiritual development. These people then became the wise souls of the community, guiding the community through important decisions. Because this happened at an older age, aging became associated with wisdom.

In fact, this is possibly the original intention for retirement. Perhaps retirement was not supposed to be a period of self-indulgence, where a person might go off and play golf and spend her saved money. Rather, perhaps it was intended to be a period where, after successfully making a living, raising a family, and building a rich set of life experiences, individuals then redirected their attention. They turned it to building their spiritual wisdom in a way that would bring their life cycle to a meaningful peak. Certainly that's how it was in many ancient cultures.

Here in our Western culture, however, we aren't taught about this stage of life, but it could still be built into our life plan. It could be that for many of us, our built-in cycles of life won't facilitate a full awakening until after we've lived a full life. I say that not to imply this is the *only* timing possible, but just to say it might be *your* timing. It was for me. So don't reject normal life in the meantime, waiting for awakening to arrive first before moving on with life. Rather, embrace life fully in all its stages.

DOING EMOTIONAL WORK

One reason living life first, before reaching awakening, might be needed, is that the challenges of life give us a chance to work through classic emotional development lessons. Doing that can be a necessary precursor to awakening. I feel all adults should make sure they work on their personal emotional issues, ones that may be deeply embedded in their psyche.

What emotional issues am I talking about? Many of us have lived through traumas or major disappointments at various stages in our lives. Such traumas are an inevitable part of life, and really, they can help define who we are in a very positive way. They can build our character and teach us a valuable range of life experiences. But those traumas, if suppressed and not addressed head-on, can also lock up our psyche in various ways, and that can prevent the free flow of personal experience and expression. So you may need to do some work to free them. Otherwise, you might continue to be blocked in life.

There are many ways to work on these issues. If you have healthy role models in your life and you have loving mentors, that may be enough—they might provide the guidance you need. Some societies even have life-stage rituals built into their culture that facilitate clearing common emotional stagnations; rituals in indigenous societies for young adults to enter manhood and womanhood are typical examples. Unfortunately, our Western societies have largely abandoned such rituals. And with the breakup of the family unit, the presence of wise and loving grandparents, ones who can perhaps guide us through our emotional trials, is now often absent. Instead, most of us need to find solutions on our own.

Many solutions are out there that directly address this. There are innumerable branches of psychology and self-development that have sprung up to address emotional problems head-on, and many work quite well. If you recognize emotional blocks in your personality, I recommend you pick one or more of these modalities and do your work. I suggest, however, that you pick a modality that has some built-in connection to the concept of awakening, rather than just jumping into, say, a Western psychoanalysis approach. That way you can coordinate your progress in both areas. I'll give a list of suggestions later in this section for emotional development modalities that also recognize awakening.

But do pick something and give it a go. Otherwise, if your psyche is locked up from emotional disturbance, it's going to make it hard for silence to flow in; there will be no space for it—the background agitation may never clear enough for silence to enter.

In fact, I'm pretty sure this was instrumental in my progress with awakening. I experienced significant emotional turmoil in my midlife. For about three years I faced a series of major traumas head-on: I had some large stresses at work where my job was being threatened, I faced the dissolution of a marriage, and I struggled with some long-festering deep-seated emotional issues that, through all this, were coming to the surface. These challenges brought to a head many of the psychological immaturities that I had kept well suppressed for decades.

Luckily, a friend led me to sources of emotional development that, over a year or so of work, addressed those issues and freed the lock they had on my psyche. It was not long after that year of emotional work that the profound silence I spoke of in Chapter 2 came on its own, even though I was not focusing in any way on awakening. I don't think that was a coincidence.

RECOMMENDED EMOTIONAL WORK MODALITIES

Here's a list of the modalities I've had positive experiences with, and so I recommend them. What I like about these is that they all incorporate the concept of the larger spiritual Self that we're all developing toward. Some even give a nod to the idea of awakening as our ultimate goal. While these are the ones I have experience with, I know there are many others that are effective.

- The Hoffman Process
- HCH-trained hypnotherapy
- Transpersonal Psychology
- Psychosynthesis
- Internal Family System
- Katie Darling's iWave Institute

You can find details on each of these by searching for these terms on the Internet.

IN CLOSING

Adding emotional work to a direct awakening focus can help you progress toward awakening. However, I think that timing and balance are also very important. There's a time when doing emotional work is the right focus, and a time when it's not. I know of people who have been doing emotional work for *decades* and who have moved the needle only slightly on the personal growth scale. They've gotten too caught up in their issues, and they've perhaps even made the issues part of their identity. In cases like that, the individual probably should be moving on to some other growth approach, or he or she should just start living life. The same applies to practicing a silence technique, or reading a lot about awakening. There's no single magic bullet to progressing in awakening. I feel you earn awakening by developing *all* aspects of your life in a well-balanced way that matches nature's timing for you. Using your intuition to find that right balance and timing is the best way to go.

To wrap up this chapter, let me say again that focusing on awakening is something you *add* to your multi-faceted life adventure, not something that replaces it. Get out there and live life, learn its lessons, and expand your life horizons in every way that you can. Do all this while also doing some work on awakening.

In the next chapter, I'm going to drill down into what I call *taking inner silence*. As I mentioned above, it's one of the key things you can add to your life to gain awakening.

5.

TAKING INNER SILENCE

After that first experience of deep and profound silence that I experienced when I closed my eyes at that fateful Thanksgiving dinner in 2012, I started taking sessions of silence again. I wanted to get that experience back, and apparently closing my eyes while staying alert was the trick to doing that. So I dusted off my old TM practice and started using it as a way to reach that silence. And it worked. In most of those new sessions where I closed my eyes using the simple TM technique, that deep and profound silence came back for much of the period.

But I also found I didn't *have* to use the TM technique. If I simply closed my eyes and looked inward, the silence was there as well. That made things simpler; heck, I could do that standing in line for an event if I wanted to. So I started doing it more and more. If I were on a plane, instead of looking for distractions in magazines, movies, or on my computer, I'd sit with my eyes closed nearly the whole flight and just feel and experience the silence. Often in the middle of the day in my home office, I'd take a break from my work and simply sit with my eyes closed and reconnect with that quiet, inner, silent being. At home before bed, instead of watching TV, I would sit for some time with my eyes closed and dwell in the silence. It felt so good and profound that I loved to repeat it.

Upon arriving in Santa Fe, I started taking even more silence. Something about this area pulled me more into it. In my quiet casita, I would spend two or three hours a day sitting with my eyes closed in silence. I would sometimes drive down into a remote desert basin southeast of the city and sit in nature taking long periods of eyes-closed silence. In the middle of the cold Santa Fe winter, I even drove to the southern part of the state where it was 70°, hiked into the bright-white gypsum sand dunes of White Sands National Monument, and sat alone in the sand for hours in deep silence. That was one of the most profound silence experiences I have had to date.

Later, I cut back from taking such long sessions of silence; it seemed less necessary over time as the silence spread into my active day. But *some* periods of silence every day still remain a central part of my practice.

Taking Silence as Key to Awakening

I've come to decide that taking periods of inner silence is not only enjoyable, but also the most important thing you can do on your path to awakening. That's because it takes you directly to that thing you want to culture as an all-time reality: silence. Whether it's two to three hours per day, like I did for a while, or just a few minutes a day, reconnecting with silence every day seems essential to me.

Taking periods of inner silence is at the core of many spiritual and religious traditions. Buddhists, Hindus, Sufis, Quakers, and many other religions have all used taking periods of pure silence as a core part of their spiritual quests.

Even mainstream lay Christianity is said to have had, at one time, a focus on taking pure silence as a part of their spiritual practice. But apparently that ended several hundred years ago, and these days you hear about pure silence being used in Christianity only within a few of their monastic organizations.

Non-religious philosophers, whether Western or Eastern, have for centuries expounded on the value of taking inner silence—it can be found in nearly all philosophical traditions.

Even *statesmen* praise the value of taking silence. For example, Ralph Waldo Emerson, a founder of America Western thinking, stated, "Let us be silent, that we may hear the whisper of God." William Penn said, "True silence is the rest of the mind, and is to the spirit what sleep is to the body, nourishment and refreshment."

The list goes on, and the idea that silence is the fundamental foundation for most of the good things in life can be found nearly everywhere. For a review of a large number of modern-day groups that use silence as their main tool of insight and spiritual development, see the recent book *The Power of Silence* by Graham Turner.

BUT HOW DO YOU DO IT?

There's no doubt in my mind that taking inner silence is key to the development of awakening. Exactly how to take periods of silence can be tricky, however. That's because it's one thing to naturally and automatically experience pure silence, but it's another thing to try to *purposefully* experience it. Experiencing inner silence, pure silence, is the most natural thing your mind can do, but at first it doesn't happen automatically. It's difficult mainly due to our life-long habits—we all have a habit, since being a baby really, of focusing exclusively on *outer* experiences, not inner ones. After all, focus on the things of the outer world is our main source of happiness. Focus on outer action is what enables us to be successful in life, to get the things we want.

But when that outer focus is overly *dominant*, it will consistently direct our attention away from inner silence and away from the benefits that inner silence can bring.

If you agree that silence is a good thing, then it makes sense to choose to *invest* in silence. That means investing some of your time and intention in making it happen. Otherwise, it probably will not come automatically. Most of us need to take purposeful actions that lead us to inner silence; we need to find ways to point the mind in that direction. One way to do that is to provide a setting in which you can regularly turn your attention away from your normal outer focus and allow your built-in capability for silence to occur. Certain forms of meditation and mindfulness provide that setting.

Meditation or Mindfulness as Taking Silence

With the right form of meditation, you can routinely experience inner silence. The meditation technique I used for decades, TM, is designed to help you experience silence. There's no doubt that my long practice of TM was a key element in my eventual growth toward awakening. Note, however, that there are also many *other* forms of meditation that can lead you to silence and awakening growth. I feel that any meditation approach that encourages you to experience deeper and deeper levels of silence during a quiet and effortless inward session can do the trick.

Another popular term these days is *mindfulness*. The term originally came from a Buddhist teaching, but it has lately been applied to a wide variety of techniques and spiritual approaches. Some of them will lead you to experiencing inner silence.

But also notice this: there are many forms of meditation and mindfulness that do *not* encourage silence. Instead, many are methods of ritual, prayer, mental focus, or intellectual pursuit. While these forms of meditation and mindfulness may have significant positive outcomes, they are not what I'm looking for in a silence session—they culture other outcomes.

As you can see, the words *meditation* and *mindfulness* are pretty generic terms these days, and they include many variations. And because many of them are *not* directed toward silence, I'm going to avoid these words from now on as the means to describe a silence session. Rather, I'm going to identify any practice in which you close your eyes and encourage silence, by the simple phrase "taking silence," so you'll mostly see *that* term from now on in this book. After all, experiencing silence is exactly what we want to be doing, and this term captures that goal quite well.

TAKING SILENCE

How do I define taking silence? To me, taking silence simply means taking a period of time where your intention and setup is to experience internal alert silence. That usually means sitting in a quiet location with your eyes closed and your mind alert. You can do this sitting in nature, in the privacy of your home, with a group of others doing the same, or even on an airplane if needed, as I mentioned in Chapter 1.

The "mind alert" aspect is important because the silence we're looking for is pure awareness or wakefulness—so you definitely want to encourage an alert mind. So for example, lying down on a bed and resting while doing it usually won't work because, out of habit and due to a natural physiological response, we tend to go into a non-alert or less alert near-sleep state at that time. Same with leaning your head back while sitting in a reclining chair. Rather, I recommend you sit with a relatively upright back and head when you do this—any normal chair will work—or even with legs crossed on the floor or on an upright couch.

Also, listening to active music or an instructional recording while trying to take silence is probably not right. The latter is often called a "guided meditation," and while there's a place for that, it's not what I have in mind here. Meditating while being physically active is also not what I have in mind. In all these cases, such activities will probably take your mind in the other direction—to awareness on objects of perception and on thoughts. The taking silence I'm talking about instead leads to a more open awareness, one not bounded by such focus or distractions.

BASIC TAKING SILENCE METHOD

Below are a few methods I suggest you consider for taking silence. I know there are many more—this is not an exclusive list—but these are ones I have experience with. I'm going to start with a method I call the Basic Taking Silence Method. I start here because it's how I meditate these days, and it emphasizes the key outcome you should be looking for: periods of clear silence in your sitting.

However, this Basic Taking Silence Method is not the method most people will use, at least not at the outset, because it assumes you can already contact that silence immediately.

That said, a small percent of you probably can use it. That may be because you have a moderate degree of silence already established in your being, and so it might come in immediately. Or perhaps that's due to previous years of meditation, or due to your life timing being just right, or because that's how you're naturally tuned.

The only way to know if this works for you is to try it, so the very basic taking-silence formula is this: find a quiet location, sit upright, close your eyes, intend to keep your mind alert, and intend to experience silence. If after closing your eyes like this, silence quickly comes flooding in and persists for at least a little while, then great, this method is for you.

UNBOUNDED AWARENESS

A question most people have at this point, however, is how do you know if you're really experiencing *silence*? What does such silence feel like; how is it experienced?

I described the sort of silence you're looking for in Chapter 2. It's being largely free of thoughts and experiencing a stillness and spaciousness, like floating on an infinite flat lake or even floating in infinite space.

The best single phrase to describe this experience is the term *unbounded awareness*. What I mean by that is your awareness is not bound by, caught up in, or locked into thoughts or other stimuli. Rather, your awareness broadens onto the flat plane of pure awareness. When that happens, stillness and mental silence click in. You'll know it when it happens because as the silence comes in strongly, you'll sense a distinct contrast.

Here's a good analogy I like to use to explain the contrast of unbounded awareness coming in. Imagine your awareness is like a flashlight that can be adjusted either to shine a very narrow beam on a small point or to project a broader light that fills much of a room. If you adjust the light so that it's a narrow beam directed toward and focused on an individual object, that's like being bound by a thought; all your awareness is caught up in a point of focus. The point of the beam (the current thought) may be shifting and changing (like moving the flashlight around a room), but it's always a point of focus at any given moment.

If instead you adjust the flashlight so that the light spreads out across an infinite visual plane, without being focused on any one thing, then that is what unbounded awareness is like. It's as if you're aware of everything at once but not of anything specific. You're only aware of your broad and unbounded awareness.

This flashlight analogy is almost exactly the description of what happens when I close my eyes to take silence daily. Within the first few moments after closing my eyes, my awareness lets go of any previous outer focus or thoughts and broadens dramatically to the unbounded still plane of silence. I'll usually sit there in that silence for some moments, enveloped in its wholeness. Then, after a short or long while, my awareness might get bound again by a new thought, which I might even get completely lost in for some moments.

And here is the basic teaching about handling such thoughts when taking silence—and it's one that is virtually the same for all good silence techniques: When I spontaneously notice that I have fully transitioned to a thought and am lost in it, I then gently favor allowing my attention to broaden again into silence. Just the intention to do that allows my awareness to release from the focused thought and spread out again to pure unbounded awareness, to pure silence. I'll go through this shift many times in my silence sessions. Or I might stay in that unbounded awareness for long periods. Or it might be a mixture that includes light, indistinct thoughts floating over the top of the silence, like small puffy clouds over a flat wide plain, all without my losing the dominant experience of stillness: silence.

That, in a nutshell, is the Basic Taking Silence Method. Is this technique for you? Well, if when you sit and close your eyes with alertness, you drop almost immediately into the experience of unbounded awareness and it persists for say five or ten seconds before thoughts come in, then this is your technique. Also, if when lost in thought you're able to come back relatively easily and promptly to that unbounded awareness, that also indicates you're ready. If you can do all that, great—this is for you.

But if that's not your experience (and for most of you it will *not* be), then no worries, just move on to the *mental vehicle* technique next. It gives you a way that, if practiced regularly, will eventually lead to the above experience.

USING A MENTAL VEHICLE TO LEAD TO SILENCE

For most of us, simply closing our eyes with alertness will not immediately lead to the experience I described above. Rather, on closing our eyes, we find ourselves immediately and consistently flooded with thoughts, images, or emotions. When I first started meditating decades ago, that happened to me—as soon as I closed my eyes, tons of thoughts flooded in and would not leave spontaneously. If that's your experience, you'll want to use a *mental vehicle* of some sort to encourage your mind to move toward silence. In fact, most people are in this situation; they can't use the basic approach I described above because enough silence is not already well established.

What do I mean by a mental vehicle? In TM and several other meditation types I know of, that vehicle is called a *mantra*—it's a meaningless sound you silently repeat whose vibrational qualities draw your attention inward toward silence. Or in other meditations, the vehicle is to follow your *breath* (typical for many Buddhist and mindfulness meditations). And in some other forms of meditation, it might be to follow an *idea* (for example, Sri Ramana Maharishi's method of repeating "Who am I?"). In each case, if used properly, the vehicle can naturally guide your mind to silence. So if you don't spontaneously experience deep silence when you close your eyes, you'll probably want to use a silence technique that uses such a vehicle.

I'll list or describe some silence techniques that use a vehicle in more detail ahead, but here's the basic technique. As above, you find a quiet location, sit upright, close your eyes, and intend to keep your mind alert. Then, very gently, bring your attention to your vehicle. Follow the vehicle lightly and allow it to disappear when it naturally does. For example, if using a mantra, repeat the mantra very gently and allow it to disappear whenever it does.

For beginners, the vehicle will usually disappear because you get lost in thoughts, and that's fine. Later, the vehicle will disappear because you're drawn into unbounded awareness, into silence. That said, don't worry if you don't experience unbounded awareness for some time. Even if you don't experience it, the process is still slowly moving your mind in that direction, which is very beneficial. It can take months or years before you really experience it clearly, and that's OK. Silence is most likely building underneath your thoughts, and someday it will break through. You are still gaining benefits in the meantime.

FORCING DOESN'T WORK

Before I list some detailed mental vehicle techniques, I want to emphasize one thing about all of them. The vehicle should be used in a very effortless way. That's so you don't strain on the technique and so you can easily and automatically transition from the vehicle to silence. You don't want to obsess on the vehicle or concentrate on it. The point is not to get caught up in the vehicle but rather just consider it as a starting point to reach your goal of silence. To ensure that, the vehicle should be used gently, in the background, and you should feel free to let it go if you lose it—whether you lose it to thoughts or silence.

The reason I mention that is the number one problem new meditators across all techniques face is trying too hard, and that usually takes the form of forcing their technique. They may do it without even realizing they're doing it. After all, in our society, most of us succeed through focus, hard work, and effort. Everything that's good seems to come from working at it, and so many of us believe that if we want more of something, we should try harder and apply more dedication.

The idea that hard work produces results is such an ingrained belief in humans that even some meditation methodologies are based on effort and manipulation. Some require holding the body in a precise and difficult posture or concentrating the mind or forcing thoughts out of the mind—or all of these things. It's as if we're imposing a penance on ourselves for years of misdeeds!

However, in my experience, *trying hard* to get to silence is a sure fire way to *prevent* it. Silence is what results when you *remove* your habit of mental effort *while staying alert*. Practices that impose effort are likely to prevent it. And such practices are difficult to keep doing week after week since so much effort is involved.

If it's so counterproductive, why do many meditation traditions use effort? I believe the effort aspect was mistakenly added somewhere in the history of their teaching. Most of these traditions were handed down over the centuries *orally*, and just like in the classic gossip game, I believe the message gradually changed to an incorrect one as it passed from ear to ear, from generation to generation. Various teachers added their opinions along the way.

In fact, there's an interesting story from one of my favorite awakening writers whose name is Adyashanti (Steven Gray). In his late teens, he started doing a Buddhist form of meditation and kept up with it diligently for fifteen years, but with little success. His technique was similar to many other Buddhist ones in which strict attention to posture and concentration was required. Finally, after he got frustrated with his lack of progress, he decided to remove all the effort-inducing elements from his meditation method, and he said that's when awakening finally started to come. He now teaches a meditation technique with zero effort and almost zero intention, and he currently preaches against the mistake of doing rigid meditation practices.

FINDING A TEACHER IS BEST

Because your initial results can often be subtle and confusing, the ideal way to learn a taking-silence technique is to find a teacher who will teach you a method and coach you through at least the beginning weeks. Such a teacher can help you in various ways. He or she can answer your questions as you get underway. He can explain experiences you may have in the sessions and that you might be wondering about. She can help you through any misunderstandings.

A teacher can also help you be patient and keep you on the proper technique. You see, because of your long habit of outer focus, it can take time to see results in these techniques. And because taking silence is such a subtle thing, when results are slow, it's easy to doubt your technique and start inserting incorrect modifications such as trying to manipulate the outcomes. A teacher can help prevent you from adding such inadvertent effort. A teacher can help you stay on track and help you gain the longer perspective needed to motivate you to keep up with the practice.

TRANSCENDENTAL MEDITATION, OR TM

I promised to go into some more detail on mental vehicle techniques you can choose. My number one recommended vehicle technique is TM.

My reason for recommending TM is not just that it's the technique I used most of my life. Rather, it's because I think it's the most *practical* technique out there. Remember, I'm encouraging you to adopt this taking silence practice along with your normal life. So whatever technique you adopt, it should be very easy to do and it should fit in with your routine. I also feel it should also be easy to find teaching and advice on it, no matter where you live.

TM matches those criteria. It's simple, very effortless, and easy to do nearly anywhere. You start at twenty minutes twice a day, which is pretty simple to fit in. Training on it is given by an organization that has certified teachers practicing in nearly every city around the world. You can probably find a teacher around the corner from you. And if later, say in another location, you feel as if you may not be meditating correctly or need advice, you simply call a local center, make an appointment, and get a free in-person meditation checking session. The technique is highly standardized, so you'll get exactly the same instructions no matter where you are.

I also feel that the advanced TM teachings are particularly powerful. They take a little bit more time to do, but it's with those advanced techniques that I felt my experiences of internal silence first really became apparent.

Also, you'll recognize immediately that TM teachers are normal everyday people; many of them have a professional career along with their TM teaching. You'll probably find that you can relate to them easily and you won't feel as if you're getting involved with someone with a cultural background very different from your culture.

To get started, just look up TM.org on the Internet.

CENTERING PRAYER

If you have a strong Christian belief system, then you may want to look into a taking-silence approach that's called the Centering Prayer. It's a process that was developed years ago by an American Benedictine priest and monk named Thomas Keating. He has been teaching and promoting it for years, and he's written many books about it.

You may be curious how something called *prayer* can be used as a silence technique, but in my opinion, the name of this technique is a misnomer. It's really not prayer in the way I think about the word, where you consciously direct requests toward a higher being. Rather, it's a technique that is not that different from TM. The difference is that instead of silently repeating a meaningless sound (the mantra), you choose the name of a Christian saint that you like, or something similar, and use that in your effortless practice. The result is similar to TM—it takes you to deep silence. I've heard many good reports about the effectiveness of this practice; using it can keep you in touch with your Christianity while you practice a technique that builds silence.

You can learn the technique by studying one of Thomas Keating's books such as *Intimacy with God* or *Open Mind, Open Heart.* Or you can find in-person instruction on the technique by going to this link: www. contemplativeoutreach.org/category/category/centering-prayer.

BREATH

Probably one of the most commonly used mental vehicles for deepening silence is to mentally follow one's breath. It's the method used in many Buddhist meditations, as well as others. Why use your breath as a vehicle? Some say that the breath is one's closest physical connection to spirit. In fact, it's said that the word *breath* comes from the root word *spirit*. The wonderful thing about following the breath to reach silence is that the breath naturally ceases automatically at the end of each breath cycle. So there's a natural letting go with each breath, which can easily lead directly to silence.

There are many book-based and online-based instructions for breath meditation. Many of the mindfulness techniques out there today use a breath-based meditation. But in my opinion, nearly all of these make it way too complicated, with too many rules. Simpler is better, and the simplest one I've found is the one at this link: www.meditationoasis.com/how-to-meditate/simple-meditations/breathing-meditations/

My criteria for a good breath technique are that it's simple and effortless, and that it does not engage the mind too much. It should not demand that you stay focused on the technique and drag your mind back to it rigidly.

If you can't find a breath technique that you like, here are some simple instructions you might want to follow. You'll see that they're very similar to the Basic Silence Technique that I described above.

First, find a comfortable place to sit upright, close your eyes, and then let your attention go to your breath. Allow your attention to effortlessly follow the breath both as it comes in and as it goes out. Don't try to manipulate the breath, just follow its natural cycle. Follow any part or aspect of the breath that your attention naturally goes to, and if that changes, let it.

When you first attempt this, because you're putting your attention on the breath for the first time, you'll probably find that you inadvertently start to manipulate your breathing. It's almost hard not to because of your new awareness on something so intimate, which you normally don't pay attention to. But don't worry, after a few minutes or a few sessions, you'll stop being self-conscious about your breath and what it's doing, and you'll follow it in a much more innocent and carefree manner.

As you follow your breath, you'll likely find that you often get lost in thought; you stop following the breath during that time. That may happen for only a few moments or for many minutes at a time. And that's fine—don't try to fight that. It's a very natural part of any silence technique. My simple instruction is, when you notice that you're lost in thought, then very gently allow your attention to move back to your breath. After a while, this will become an automatic process and it won't seem like such a big deal.

You may find at the end of an exhalation that your awareness is on the stillness and silence that are naturally present for a moment at the end of a breath. Congratulations—you're starting to experience silence in your sessions. You may even find that you stop breathing for a few moments or more at that point. If that happens, just allow it to happen—but don't try to make it happen. Or you may sense that the silence comes in independently from the breath cycle, along with it, so to speak. Or you may detect no silence at all; it may seem as if you're just either aware of breath or thoughts. You may be drawn to different aspects of the breath, in different parts of your body.

All of these possibilities are fine—don't try to manipulate the outcome; rather, allow any experiences to come as they do. Your single instruction is as above: When you notice that you're lost in a thought, then very gently allow your attention to move back to your breath. That's your only job, and even then, be very easy with that instruction. Don't feel as if you have to watch for being lost in a thought or attend to it as a chore. Just happily enjoy the thought while lost in it, and then happily return to watching the breath when you notice you're no longer lost in thought.

VARIATIONS OF TAKING SILENCE

I just listed four simple methods of taking silence, and there are many more out there. So choose one and practice it. If you already have an effortless technique that is similar, go with it. No matter which technique you use, eventually—over days, weeks, or months of practice—you'll notice more and more silence coming in at various parts of the session. Silence may come and stay present during each session for days or weeks at a time and then leave for days or weeks at a time. Or it may even take years for you to really notice it. Don't get discouraged; whatever comes is the natural outcome for you.

I mentioned previously that in my first years of TM, it was the outer benefits that kept me going because the experience during practice itself seemed unimpressive. I'm glad I kept going because later the experiences in the practice became quite profound. So here's my advice: Pick a taking-silence technique and just keep up with the practice.

BRINGING SILENCE INTO ACTIVITY

The real goal of taking silence is to carry that silence spontaneously into activity. By becoming familiar with silence intimately in your repeated silence sessions, you create a habit of carrying that silence with you all the time. When silence is present in activity, it supports you and penetrates everything you do in a positive way. The real meaning of awakening, enlightenment, is to have silence be a nearly full-time presence in your life.

So one thing you may want to do just before getting up from a silence session is to set the intention that the silence you experience in the session will continue into your activity. Immediately after a session, make a very slight intention to notice how the silence lingers into your activity. Notice how it feels as it continues in the background along with your outer activity and thoughts. To me, this is the true practice of mindfulness: to be aware of the silence already there—not to try to artificially force a witnessing of your thoughts and life, but rather to notice it when it's naturally present.

SILENCE RETREATS

After practicing your new silence sessions for some weeks or months, I highly recommend adding weekend or week-long silence retreats to augment your daily practice. This is optional, but the benefits of taking silence retreats are great. There's something very profound that happens when you can get away from the hustle and bustle of your daily work and family life and dive deeply for long periods of time into silence. In such a retreat, depending on who's leading it, you either take many more of your short sessions per day or you extend the length of each of your sessions or both. The long exposure to silence is usually mixed with lectures or readings about the silence method, awakening, or related topics.

What I find during these retreats is that even during times I'm not actually in a period of inner silence, I can feel as though I'm imbedded in the silence. The silence can last all day long. Taking such retreats will multiply the effect of your daily practice many times over. Because of that, nearly every organization that teaches a form of silence or meditation also offers such retreats, and I encourage you to take advantage of them. I have no doubt that some of my biggest advances in experiencing silence came as a result of such retreats. Taking a long weekend's retreat every couple months or even a week long retreat every year or so can have phenomenal results. And to me, they are the ideal form of vacation because they truly are rejuvenating. I recall returning to work from these with a newfound energy and interest in work and life.

You'll probably want to find a retreat that matches your silence approach. It's nice to take extended silence with a group practicing a similar approach to yours because you can enjoy the camaraderie and shared experiences. You can learn from one another. There's also a group consciousness effect that occurs when you take silence together with others of like mind, and that effect multiplies the results of the retreat—so take advantage of that.

As I said, nearly all organizations that teach a form of silence growth also offer these retreats. For example, the TM organization—the organization I'm most familiar with—offers retreats regularly. After you learn the basic TM technique, you can take these retreats any time; just ask your teacher to notify you when such a retreat is scheduled in your area. There is of course a fee for these retreats, as they're often located in a pleasant resort or hotel settings with food provided.

The best deals on TM retreats are those offered to advanced TM meditators. Once you progress to the TM-Sidhis program, you can join an ongoing retreat located at the TM facility in Fairfield, Iowa, and it's free (at least it was at the time of this writing). All you need to do is arrange and pay for food and lodging nearby—something inexpensive in that small Midwestern town. I have done many of these Fairfield retreats for a week or more at a time, and I find the experience to be hugely rewarding—sometimes even life changing. For example, a few years ago I felt stuck in a lull of my growth in silence. So I attended a weeklong retreat in Fairfield, joining the thousands of others that are typically there in group meditation, and by the time I left a week later, my silence in life had deepened profoundly.

In Closing: Regular Practice

No matter which silence technique you choose to use, once you have an effortless silence method in place, then use your method to take silence regularly. I started out at twenty minutes, twice a day, and increased it from there. You can do less or more; just do what's comfortable and what feels right or what your teacher advises you to do, and stick with it every day. If you keep up with your daily practice, you'll find that over time, the silence begins to grow in your awareness—and that is a major part of the path to awakening.

6.

A Purposeful Life Guided by Intuition

All my life I have taken seriously the intuitive and psychic capabilities of others. On and off I've met people who've had that capacity in one form or another, and I've generally found those people to be honest and sincere. Many of them I've found to be exceptionally *accurate*. I'm sure there are some fakes out there, and the lay press just loves to emphasize those. But we have fake doctors out there too, yet we don't debunk the entire medical industry. So yes, I do believe that intuition and psychic abilities are real and that most people who offer them are good and honest people.

I always assumed, however, that you had to be *born* with the gift, and if you weren't and wanted it—well, *too bad*. I certainly didn't think *I* could significantly develop those capabilities, even though I sometimes saw some small glimpses of intuition even within myself.

But with the onset of simple awakening and the underlying silence, I found that my own intuition began to develop rapidly and in remarkable ways. In the last three years, I've seen example after example of how my own intuition has grown stronger and stronger and how it's now guiding me, nearly always, to just the right things.

I could tell you many stories of such instances that have occurred over those three years, but perhaps most interesting are the detailed circumstances of my move to Santa Fe, New Mexico. In Chapter 2, I talked a little about how I found the special writing location in Santa Fe, the place where I wrote this book. But there is, in fact, a lot more to the story of those circumstances, and it's a story of pure intuitive guidance. So let's go back and visit the very beginning of my Santa Fe journey.

THE STORY OF MOVING TO SANTA FE

My initial hints that I was supposed to do something major in Santa Fe started way back in the fall of 2013, a full year before my first visit. My brothers and I were planning our next weeklong annual retreat for the following fall. Out of the blue, I suggested we do it in Santa Fe. I have no idea why I brought it up—I hadn't traveled there for decades and I wasn't reading about it or thinking about it in any way. Our family had a very old connection to that area, but that was long past. So for whatever reason, Santa Fe came up in my mind, and based on our old family ties, my brothers and I agreed it would make a good trip. So we scheduled it for the following year.

Five months later I started planning that trip, and every time I brought up information about Santa Fe on the Internet or in travel books, I kept getting inner impulses of familiarity and recognition. Some sort of quiet internal bell would go off in the back of my mind each time I studied that location. None of it was logical; our family connections to the area had ceased back in the 1950s, and no ties remained. But over the weeks of on-and-off research in my free time, I began to feel a magnetic pull to the place. That pull continued to grow, and soon I found that I couldn't read or study enough about Santa Fe—I wanted to learn more and more. I was even compelled to get on Google's Street View photo feature and visually "walk" up and down the streets of Santa Fe to try to figure out what was grabbing me about the place.

As the weeks went by and the impulses grew, I started thinking that maybe I should spend some significant time there; something was obviously very special about this place for me. I even started daydreaming about where I would live if I were to have a second home there. I studied maps and photos, and I identified, really just by feel, a specific section off Canyon Road that seemed right for me. But when I priced rentals there on the Internet, they were ridiculously expensive and everyone wanted a year's commitment. I knew it would be a stretch to rent there a full year *and* keep my place in California at the same time, so I dismissed the notion as senseless daydreaming.

A month later, out of the blue, I received a note from my long-lost old friend Lance Eaves saying that he had moved to Santa Fe a year earlier and that I should come for a visit. Boy, what a coincidence! But I made no commitments to visit him because I still didn't see how this was going to work in the long run or where it would get me. In spite of that, my impulse to visit there continued to get stronger, and finally I couldn't stay away. So as I explained in Chapter 2, I jumped in my car and drove from California to Santa Fe, completely on a whim and in the moment. I justified my actions by calling it a writing trip, but I also wanted to visit long enough to see why my impulse to spend time there was so strong— it seemed as if it were about more than just writing.

As I also explained in Chapter 2, when Lance heard I was coming, he told me he was out of town but he invited me to use his casita apartment to do some writing. When I arrived, I was blown away to learn that his casita was in the *exact* area of Santa Fe that I had identified earlier as being where I might want a home. And not only did I discover the apartment was a writer's muse, but I also discovered I *knew* the apartment manager who let me into Lance's apartment. When I say I "knew" her, I don't mean that I had a previous acquaintance with her; I didn't. Rather, I mean that the moment we met, I just felt I *knew* her—as if we'd been longtime friends.

Her name was Glenys Carl, and she was a lovely woman a bit older than me. She was originally from Wales and spoke with a delightful Welsh accent. She had deep silver gray hair, bright sparkling blue eyes, and an inner glow that was full of light. Thin and wispy and ethereal, she was nearly angelic in appearance. I learned that she had founded and now operated a nonprofit organization in Santa Fe that arranged free hospice care for those that needed it—so both by career and character, she really *was* a saint. She was also one of the published authors who had written a book in that very same casita years earlier, and so she deeply understood the magic of the place for writing.

Arriving there told me many things at a quiet, intuitive level. For one thing, it wasn't just Santa Fe that I was attracted to. As soon as I crossed into New Mexico, I started to sense the silence of the land in the entire state. That silence resonated with the silence growing in me. And while Santa Fe itself is moderately busy—it is, after all, the capital city of New Mexico—it too had its silent resonance. I sensed that various parts of the city vibrated in consonance with the deeper history of the land and that somehow I had a tie to that.

I had only planned on staying three or four days on this quick drop-in visit, so as soon as I could, I set up my laptop in Lance's back yard and began writing. That's when the magic started and the book that had been stalled for so long started to pour out of me. My intuition and creative floodgates opened. It was as if all the barriers lifted and the story I was supposed to tell found its outlet in that atmosphere.

At the end of those two days, I had the book well underway. I had most of the first chapter written, and I had ideas for the structure of the rest of the book. I was blown away! I decided I just had to find a place in Santa Fe that I could rent and come and go to, to continue to write. Wouldn't it be fantastic if I could find something in that same casita complex? But apartments are almost impossible to find in this section of Santa Fe, and they are typically quite expensive—I'm not the first person to discover the charm of this historical area.

So when I asked Glenys, I expected her to shake her head sadly and say no. But instead, she stared at me in surprise and said, "Didn't Lance tell you? He's moving out in a few weeks, and I haven't looked for another renter yet, so you can have his place if you want." I felt the earth move a bit when she announced that. There's no doubt in my mind that the impulse that made me jump in my car and drive that week to that location was all a part of some deep intuitive guidance.

Now here's another amazing aspect of this story. When Glenys offered the place to me, I told her that I probably couldn't organize my life to come back for several months; I had too many things going on in California that I had to attend to. When I told her that, she looked at me and said the most remarkable thing. She said, "You're supposed to write your book here, and I will hold this place for you until you can come." How did she know that? How could she know that moments before, I had decided I *was* supposed to write my book there, *this* book. And why would Glenys hold it for me and risk lost rent for a person she barely knew? After all, we'd only talked for a few moments. It's clear to me that my intuition had guided me to the right place, to meet the right person, at exactly the right time.

In fact, not only did Glenys offer to hold the apartment for me, but she offered to rent it on a month-to-month basis in case I couldn't handle a full-time rental for a full year. She offered a monthly price that was about half of the going rate in that area. All of those facts combined to make my decision to do my writing in just the perfect spot a very easy one. You see, I was still conflicted about writing the book, and I might not have done it otherwise. Glenys was inspired to make me an offer I could not refuse, and I was inspired to show up at the right place and at the right time to receive it. I guess you could say that *my* intuition, *Glenys's* intuition, and *fate* were all working together on this project.

After about six months of on-and-off visits to Santa Fe, I decided I had to move there permanently. Really, inside my heart I knew from my very first arrival in New Mexico that it would happen, but it was hard to bring that knowledge to the surface and admit it. After all, I was in a happy relationship with a lovely woman who was tied to California. I was a California native who'd sworn I'd never leave again. I knew almost no one in Santa Fe, and I had no *logical* reason to move there. But I did move there, this book got written, and in a way, New Mexico has captured me.

As the weeks and months went by, it was obvious why I was supposed to be there, beyond writing this particular book. A deep connection and bond began forming between Northern New Mexico and me that is still developing as I write this. There's something about the *land* here, for me, that intrigues and nurtures me, and that makes me want to discover more. I now take multiday journeys in my 4WD Jeep Wrangler into various hidden canyons and mountain areas, and into rarely visited small villages. I have found numerous spiritually pristine—nearly *holy*—places here that few living in the state know of. I find myself explaining to locals about favorite destinations tucked into corners only miles away—unknown to them. It's as if the state is inviting me in and unlocking her secrets for me in an intimate and loving way.

I find it all deeply moving and stirring to my soul. There's a silence in the land here that resonates with my particular brand of internal silence and enlivens it in profound ways. And the vastness of the open unspoiled vistas here expands the vastness and the infinite nature of my soul. Major writing inspirations arise on almost every trip I take in this state, and these are inspirations I have never found anywhere else. It's clear that my next books, and my next life adventures, are being percolated here in Northern New Mexico.

A REGULAR OCCURRENCE

This story of being guided by intuition to my New Mexico writing place—and my new home—is in no way an isolated instance. Example after example of intuition guiding me to just the right things began happening over and over again as simple awakening rolled in. I found myself consistently inspired to be in the right place at the right time to make the right things happen, not only in personal matters but also in business matters. And that's how things seem to go now, over and over again as simple awakening has set in for me. Intuition has now become a deep and trusting guide to nearly everything I do. In fact, at this point in my awakening journey, I can safely say that fully 80 to 90 percent of my daily actions and life decisions are being guided by intuition.

The advantage of using this intuition is that it leads me to positive outcomes that I never would have *reasoned* my way to before. It removes the struggle of figuring out all of life's steps. It's a major reason I have such a growing feeling of ease and freedom with the growth of simple awakening: next steps are so often simply presented to me. And ultimately, it almost always works better than the alternative: logic and emotional decision making.

Note, however, that intuition is a very subtle thing, and learning how to use it can be hard at first. Except in very rare cases, it doesn't shout out at you or even talk to you at a normal conversational level. Rather, it comes in the form of a subtle knowing, often so subtle that at first it's easy to miss. It can take a while to get accustomed to using it.

TYPES OF INTUITION

There are various types of intuition; the kind of intuition I'm referring to in my awakening process is a distinct kind that seems to have a distinct purpose. First, let me tell you what it is *not*. The intuition developed through awakening is not the same as psychic awareness. I don't use this intuition to predict the future for myself or others. And I don't use it to talk to the departed. Psychic abilities like that are wonderful gifts that some people have, but that's distinct and different from this intuition I'm referring to.

Furthermore, this intuition is not something I use to answer random questions. It won't help me ace my final social studies exam—I can't ask questions such as what is the capital of Madagascar and get the answer back. And unfortunately, it's unlikely I'll use this intuition to pick winning lottery numbers.

So if this intuition is not about psychic abilities or filling ad hoc requests, what good is it? The intuition you gain from silence and from awakening has a very specific role: to gently (or firmly) nudge you in the direction of your life purpose. Its role is all about guiding you down your optimal life path. The intuition that comes with awakening is there to eventually lead you to your highest good. Ultimately, I feel that is much better than answering ad hoc questions or having psychic insights.

This doesn't mean that this intuition is *always* about profound topics or major life decisions. Once it rolls in, you won't feel as if every insight has a life-changing impact. Rather, more often you'll get guidance on day-to-day decisions, small steps on your life path, all of which eventually add up to reaching your highest good.

This intuition comes to me at a very subtle level of thought or feeling, one that may not be particularly distinct from all my other thoughts or emotions. For that reason, intuition was at first very easy for me to miss. Even now, it comes as a very quiet feeling or knowing inside. I just know something is right—or not right—not because my logic tells me, not even because a thought forms that says, "This is right." But simply because I *know* it, often well below the level of conscious thought. Because it comes at such a quiet level, that's probably the reason I can't abuse it, say, for using it to choose a lottery number if that's not on my path. That's because as soon as my mental state becomes too disrupted (which is what happens if I veer off my path), I lose the intuitive input.

I've shared how, with my growth of silence in awakening, a very quiet level of awareness got established nearly permanently. When I learned to work and act from that quiet level, that's when intuition started to flow steadily. With practice, and over time, I got accustomed to using it consistently. As I said, these days I use it nearly *all* the time.

SOME HISTORY

As I mentioned, it wasn't always this way for me. I had small glimpses in the past but nothing major. I first started noticing some minor intuitive insights shortly after I started meditating many decades ago, but to a very limited degree. It wasn't so much that I noticed the intuitional input itself and said, "Wow, I just got an intuitional hit!" Rather, I noticed that life events that were quite beneficial to me were occurring on and off, and I often traced them back to my having acted on very minor hunches. It didn't happen regularly, so it was almost impossible to predict which hunch would pay off. And I couldn't make it happen on demand. In fact, it was so rare that I certainly didn't consider myself an intuitive person.

After I enrolled in the more advanced TM course called the TM-Sidhis, I found intuition increased a bit more. The typical way I'd use intuition was when I needed to make a decision. In such a case, I'd purposely get quiet for a moment and turn my attention inward slightly. It's not that I'd close my eyes, but rather I'd remove my focus from anything outside and look inside somewhat, as when thinking or daydreaming. I'd then wait for a knowing, often get one, and I'd go with it.

Over the years, I found that more and more of those decisions turned out to be correct—and that's when I first started to take intuition seriously as a useful and reliable gift. The reason I think the TM-Sidhis increased intuition is that with the *sidhis*, I found silence in activity started to arrive a bit. Fast forward to the most recent three years, and the silence in activity has increased dramatically. That's coincident with intuition really taking off, so there's no doubt in my mind that silence and intuition are deeply linked.

It makes sense that silence and intuition *should* be linked. If silence is established in you to the degree that you notice it throughout the day, those things associated with silence should increase. Think about the discussion in Chapter 2—what I postulated silence is. I stated that, at its purest, silence is the unmanifest field of infinite potential underneath all of existence. If you believe that theory, then you know silence should have access to perfect information. If you function from silence throughout the day, you *should* have access throughout the day to critical knowledge that supports you.

No More Focus on Fear or Concern

But admittedly, that theory can be bit of a leap to accept, so let me submit another explanation for why intuition grows with silence and awakening.

One of the very distinct things I noticed with the growth of silence and awakening is that my fear-based and concern-based thinking went away almost completely. I found myself no longer driven by large or small fears or concerns throughout the day, whether they were economic fears, social concerns, safety fears, or health concerns—nearly all went by the wayside. It wasn't until they left that I realized how much they had dominated my thinking. I'm convinced that nearly everyone is driven by such fear-based or concern-based thoughts, often below the surface of our conscious minds. With the growth of awakening, I found they no longer occupied my hour-to-hour or day-to-day background thoughts.

Of course fears and concerns still arise for me, momentarily, when appropriate. If I approach a dangerous intersection on a highway, for example, I do so with alert awareness. If there's a big truck coming at me, in the moment, I experience the appropriate fear and swerve!

But it's the background self-talk that goes on all day long for most of us that has reduced most dramatically for me. Most of us have these thoughts throughout the day. Thoughts about whether you look good, whether people will like you, whether you're doing the right thing, whether you'll get that next big sale, whether your kids are safe, whether you're pleasing your boss, how angry you are at that person, whether you have enough money coming in to buy what you want, whether your job is secure, whether a certain person is doing what you want—phew! And these are only a few examples of the slew of fear- or anger-based thoughts that occupy most people's minds most of the time, either at the mind's surface or just below the surface.

Thoughts like that require a lot of energy and attention. Some estimates say that the average person has sixty thousand thoughts per day and that 80 percent of them are negative! Think of all the energy that goes into that.

In contrast, imagine if such background negative self-talk were gone. I assert that having such a quiet state would open up your mind to receive the quieter messages silence sends you to guide your life in a positive direction—messages you now miss. In fact, a case could be made that, from our moment of birth, we all have a constant stream of useful but quiet guidance coming but we can't hear it through the fear-based thinking we constantly have. So this is one explanation of why awakening makes intuition work by removing the steady onslaught of noisy self-talk.

In fact, as awakening sets in and you trust your intuition more and more, you'll find that *you think less in general*. Just as with silence coming into your meditations and having fewer thoughts there, as silence comes into your *activity* you have fewer thoughts there as well. In awakening, you find that you don't need a steady stream of thoughts to continually define who you are—silence is who you are. If the idea of fewer thoughts bothers you, then let me ask you, what do you need all those thoughts for anyway? If you've got a steady flow of quiet knowing that guides your activity safely, accurately, and joyfully, why do you need to constantly be analyzing and regurgitating things?

Don't get me wrong, if you're in the middle of a project that requires thinking, you think. And I've found that the kind of thinking I need for such work has become much more powerful because it's not distracted by so much other noise—it's become more purposeful. Random thoughts do still arise much of the time, but most of those thoughts are about positive things like something to put in my next book or how to help someone I see having an issue. Almost zero are complaints about circumstances, fears about outcomes, or worries about myself.

What I've also found with growing awakening is that as I'm *experiencing* things—nature, people, my surroundings—I do so more directly and with much less mental interpretation that filters the experience. This change is huge. About a year ago I realized I was seeing my surroundings much more clearly and with little judgment. The result is that I experience life more fully, more richly, more deeply, and more accurately. I'm no longer constantly interpreting everything and calculating my next steps or judging impacts on my well-being. I'm just experiencing.

INTUITION VERSUS LOGIC

As I said, intuition is a very subtle thing, and you may not even know it's going on at first. One indication that intuition is at play is that you start seeing outcomes of very minor decisions turn out to be very good for you. Life starts going very well as you follow your gut.

But if life goes well for you most the time anyway, how do you know *intuition* is what's guiding that? Maybe you're just a lucky person. Or maybe you're a *smart* person.

I want to talk about smartness for a moment, and in so doing, yet again I'm going to talk a bit more about New Mexico. My father was a nuclear physicist. In fact, he was one of the handful of nuclear physicists that designed the first atomic bomb while working on the Manhattan Project in Los Alamos, New Mexico, during World War II. I have four brothers who were born here in Northern New Mexico while my dad was on that project. I'm the youngest and I was *conceived* here, but I was born in Berkeley, California, after my dad wrapped up his bomb work in New Mexico and returned to Berkeley to complete his doctorate. So you could say my recent move to New Mexico is a homecoming of sorts. Since I now think I'll live in New Mexico for the remainder of my life, my move here is in a way a closing of a lifelong circle.

But getting back to my father, with his nuclear physics background, you might expect that my dad was a pretty smart guy, and in fact, he was; I feel he was one of the smartest persons I've ever known. Mostly, he was a very *logical* person. I grew up in a household where logic reigned supreme. We were taught that everything should be thought through carefully. In particular, I was taught that you usually couldn't trust your emotions when making decisions, that they could lead you astray. A logical life-approach got ingrained in my early life, so I understand logical thinking well!

In fact, trusting primarily logic and science is pretty typical for my father's generation. The growing reliance on logic and science over superstition and old worn-out traditions is one of the things that characterizes the advancement of society after the Dark Ages and into recent history. To this day, as a society we tend to trust science and logic, and we tend to discount non-logic-based thinking.

It's good to discount non-logic-based thinking if it's fear-based, jealousy based, competition based, or something similar, because such thinking usually leads to poor outcomes. Even thoughts coming from positive passions can often be from the wrong place ("I have to buy that red sports car today!"). So it makes sense not to trust all impulses like these, and in many cases, you *do* need to rely on logic. Logic rises above those impulses.

But once awakening starts to set in, that changes because the guidance from the intuition of awakening *is* trustworthy. You see, it's the fact that most of us are living life in a *non-awakened* state that makes using logic so necessary. It's our disconnected state that drives us to using logic so often in decisions. It's because we can't trust our disconnected and random impulses that we allow logic to reign supreme—it's all we have.

In contrast, if your decisions are coming from *connection to silence*, then non-logical decisions *can* be trusted; in fact, they usually *trump* logic. Decisions coming directly from pure silence—pure awareness—are much more powerful and accurate than any logical analysis could ever be. As you start to grow in awakening, as silence starts to move into your awareness, you'll have more and more successful intuitive events, and that trust will grow.

For me, in its first stages, that was admittedly a bit of a struggle. To come from such an intensely logical basis of thinking all my life, full circle, to a totally intuitive basis of thinking—what a contrast! It's a very pleasant contrast, but one that took some work to get to.

GETTING STARTED WITH INTUITION

Should you immediately start trusting all your whims? No. My recommendation, based on my slow transition to intuitive thinking, is to take this slowly and step by step. I did it very slowly as silence and simple awakening developed.

At first, I found it was often hard to distinguish between intuitive knowing and regular thinking. Only the outcome told me which was which. Over time, however, I became more confident in telling such thinking apart as impulses arose. There's no way I can describe to you precisely how to distinguish them. Really, all you can do is practice and slowly gain trust. The way I gained that trust was, if I had a thought or knowing to do something, I'd say to myself, "I'm going to go with that and see what happens." Over time as positive outcomes resulted more and more, I learned to recognize the manner in which the intuitive impulses came up and how to distinguish them from regular thoughts that usually were less successful.

One thing I noticed after awakening progressed and I saw intuition working for me was that when making decisions, my *first* impulses were often the *right* ones. You see, the intellect takes a few moments to kick in and introduce doubt or contrary instructions. So I found that if I could catch my knowing before that happened, the outcomes were often more successful.

In fact, about two years ago, after onset awakening was significantly advancing, I got so confident from witnessing positive outcomes that I made a rather wild decision. I decided that when making day-to-day choices, I would *always* go with my first knowing and see what happened. I committed, at least for a while, to no longer analyzing the decision but to acting on my first impulse. What happened? I found the results to be amazing—I almost never regretted a decision made that way. Of course, with very important decisions, I allowed the intellect to air its concerns. And if the intellect made an especially compelling case, and if my intuitive knowing did not present a strong counter-case, I went with the intellect. But amazingly, my intellect wasn't needed that often in day-to-day decisions.

GREAT FREEDOM

Think of what I just described. These days, due to my steady trust and use of intuition, I rarely question my first impulses; rather, I almost always go with my initial guidance. In fact, after a while, I found I stopped asking questions such as "Should I do this?" or "Should I do that?" Instead, I found that the impulse to act appropriately was there before the question arose. Think of that. Think of the freedom and ease of living that brings. To be able to just go with life by following your consistent and gentle guidance at all times—that *really* brings joy to life! This is what happens when intuition sets in nearly full time; this is what happens with growing awakening.

In fact, I feel that much of the angst and stress that most people feel in life is due to their trying to actively and consciously work around problems. I truly think most of us create many of our own problems by making poor unconnected decisions that then spin off into negative consequences down the road—it becomes a vicious cycle. But once silence sets in, awakening starts growing, and intuition kicks in nearly full-time, not only do your initial decisions become more accurate, but as a result, you also spend a lot less energy trying to undo the outcomes of your previous bad ones.

LIFE PURPOSE AND DESTINY

I want to get back to my original definition of intuition and explain it more. This will explain why, in my discussion about intuition, I say that awakening-based intuition is always *right*.

Recall I stated that awakening-based intuition is a gentle guide that nudges you in the direction of actions that help you complete your life purpose—actions that lead you to your highest good. But, you may ask, why must intuition be focused on your life purpose and highest good? Why *can't* you use it to, say, pick the winning roulette table number or beat somebody at Scrabble? To answer that question opens a set of discussions about *destiny*.

Whether our lives are predestined to any degree or not is a controversial subject. So I need to state that this section on destiny is based almost completely on theory and on my personal beliefs. What I'm about to say I have absolutely no proof of. Rather, the ideas come from my own intuition, my experience, and from my reading the books of others that I intuitively recognize as being true.

In particular, the author Michael Newton has works I find very useful. Michael Newton is a hypnotherapist who worked for decades in private practice as a psychological counselor, addressing the needs of tens of thousands of clients over his career. Using hypnotherapy to regress his adult clients into their childhood, he often discovered early traumas that were psychological blocks for those clients—blocks that could be released with hypnotherapy. Michael states in his book *The Journey of Souls* that years ago, when regressing a client to his childhood, he discovered he had regressed the client further, actually into a past life.

Michael says he had no interest in metaphysics or spirituality; in fact, he was an atheist and didn't believe in past lives. So he at first dismissed these past-life regression experiences as misunderstandings or subconscious artifacts. However, after months and years of similar results with many clients, he said he could no longer dismiss those results. They were too consistent and also too useful for helping heal his clients.

Then Michael discovered that he could regress his clients to the period of time *in between lives*. In other words, he took them to the time when the person was a soul on the "other side," planning out his or her next life. Again, he at first dismissed those results, but he later came to trust them and found those sessions to be powerful tools to help counsel clients on why their current life was the way it was and how to improve on it. He then made it his mission to fully explore, through regressing his clients, life as a soul on the other side: how we operate there and how we plan out our future lives there.

He wrote about all this in two books; the first as I mentioned is called *The Journey of Souls*, and the second is called *The Destiny of Souls*. Both books are extremely informative and quite eye-opening. Michael is a scientist at heart, and he accepts his rather amazing findings only with skepticism—in fact, it's his skepticism and his subsequent fact-checking that makes the books so believable. If you've ever wondered about these topics, I recommend both these books highly.

From Michael Newton's works and others', and from my own intuition, this is what I believe: I believe that each of us has a life plan, you might say a *life purpose*. I believe it was established before we were born—while we were souls on the other side, planning this lifetime. Those plans establish what major life experiences we will have—experiences that will help us learn, grow, and advance in this lifetime.

The life plan, by the way, is consistent with the plans of life partners and with our place and role in the larger framework of the universe; that's because on the other side during that planning, we have insights into all of that and coordinate with it. We may even coordinate our plan with a life partner's plan before we arrive. I believe this plan kicks in at our birth and then gets played out as we move through time in our life. So as you can see, you might say I believe we all have a *destiny*.

I also believe there's a lot of leeway in the plan, that there's a range of probable outcomes already established before we come. There's a main path that will lead to our most intended outcome. But by using free will, we can diverge from it to a certain extent. You might say that from any given moment, there are other branches of probable outcomes that extend into the future.

Think of a tree lying on its side, with the base of the tree to the left representing your birth date and time moving to the right. The trunk and branches represent possible life events over time. The main trunk is your primary planned life path, and there are branches out from that path that indicate less likely or less ideal paths. With free will, we can choose these others. The others may still produce good results; they just might not be the best ones or the initially desired plans. Some can even be rather nasty paths—again, due to our free will, we may make choices in life that can lead to any of these.

While the main path is our planned path, it's not necessarily a complete bed of roses. Rather, we purposely plan challenges on even our best path, ones that build character. And if you believe in the concept of past-life karma, then I'll also add that we build in events in this life that balance out the actions of previous lives.

Again, this is a personal belief of mine and you don't have to buy it to grow toward awakening. But the concepts are helpful, particularly to understand why intuition works and is so important. You see, at some deep place inside you, you *know* your life plan and its details. It's obviously not in your conscious awareness, but it's stored deeply inside you. The key is that you access it with intuition. If you access it consistently, moment by moment, as happens with awakening, then you consistently follow your divinely planned life. If in an unconnected state you miss your moment-to-moment cues, then you follow less optimal probable paths.

As I said, your primary plan is coordinated with the greater plan of the universe. You might say that your plan is ecologically optimal in the sense that, in a complex and unfathomable way, it fully interrelates with the optimal plans of all other human beings and of all of nature. So if you follow your plan (by following your intuition), you're doing the highest good for yourself and for the world. Imagine if all individuals, especially business and government leaders, were tuned in to those plans!

Again, if you're awakened or near it, your optimal plan is accurately executed through your moment-to-moment intuitive decisions. You don't see and think the whole plan through ahead of time. For example, you don't download your plan for the coming year in one sitting, write it down, and then work hard to meet it. With awakening, it's usually a moment-to-moment flow.

That said, if you do get inspired to write down a goal on awakening (and you might), then such goals *are* life-plan-derived (usually without your knowing that). But even then, the work you do toward that goal (meaning the actions you take) is usually inspired in the moment, guiding you with intuition toward your life purpose.

IN CLOSING

So intuition is the knowing you have, from moment to moment, that guides you along your life plan. With growing awakening, you become more and more aware of that knowing, and so you can more easily follow your plan to an optimal outcome. This is one of the reasons life often becomes much easier in awakening: with intuition, your decisions become much more automatic and fruitful.

I mentioned that you're not consciously aware of your life plan, that it's stored deep inside you. So you may be wondering, where inside you is your plan stored? Is it in your subconscious mind? Is it stored in some spiritual plane? And how is it delivered to you at just the right time? To answer these questions and more, we need to talk about the concept of the *higher self*. That's what the next chapter is all about.

7.

THE WISDOM OF YOUR HIGHER SELF

The presence of a higher self is something that started to grow in my awareness a few years ago. Discussing it, though, really brings me to a discussion of *spirit*.

After more permanently moving to Santa Fe in the Spring of 2015, my appreciation of New Mexico changed and deepened. I decided that the "something" I sensed under the surface of this place could only be described as *spirit*. I've tried to avoid using the word *spirit* in this book mainly because it often implies a connection to a spiritual *personality* of some sort, perhaps even to a spiritual *being*. Such a discussion too quickly brings the book into a religious context, and that's definitely *not* the kind of spiritual awakening I've been having. But as I've lived full-time in New Mexico over the months, I'm discovering that there *is* a personality of a sort in the energy that underlies New Mexico. And it has been a pleasure to get to know it.

New Mexico has more Native American Pueblos and reservations than any other state in the country. Santa Fe, for example, is almost completely surrounded by Indian settlements, and their influence is a deep part of the character of the city. The downtown historic plaza of Santa Fe is known for its large number of Indians who sell their handmade jewelry there every day. Native American art and jewelry are also sold in half the stores on the plaza. There's an Indian arts museum that sits a block off the plaza. Nearby, just off Canyon Road, is a large School for Advanced Research complex devoted to studying Indian anthropology. A thousand yards east of there the massive Museum of Indian Arts & Culture resides on Museum Hill. A bit south of the plaza is the Santa Fe Indian school complex, owned and operated by the nineteen Pueblos of New Mexico to educate Native Americans. And many other similar Native American institutions are scattered around the city. Drive in any direction and you can't help seeing that Native American culture permeates the entire city and region.

Now of course, there's more than just the *Indian* culture in New Mexico. Perhaps even more visible in downtown Santa Fe are remnants of the *Spanish* culture that date back centuries. Santa Fe was founded as a Spanish government center years before the pilgrims arrived on the east coast of America, and most of the oldest structures here are either remaining from, or a reflection of that long-ago era. Historic Spanish churches and chapels are everywhere in New Mexico, many with a distinctive Spanish architecture.

Later, when New Mexico was merged with the United States as a territory, Anglos moved in and brought their classic Southwestern ranching and cowboy culture to the area. And then in the 1920s, Santa Fe and Taos became centers for artists, which has also influenced the magic of the area ever since. All of those influences have combined to create a distinct and tangible sense of roots in this region that has not faded. That strong culture is not only *visible* in the architecture, food, and place names, but it can be felt; I can sense it everywhere.

For me, out of all the various historical influences I just described, what I sense primarily is the ancient Native American one. I'm most moved by the thousand-year-old Indian ruins that dot the landscape of New Mexico. For example, just northwest of Santa Fe are a number of famous ancient cliff dwellings that are now part of Bandelier National Monument; you can hike through and explore them. The extensive Chaco Canyon Indian ruins that sit at the Western edge of New Mexico are known as the oldest of the ancestral Pueblo Indian centers. Chaco Canyon is remarkable for its intelligent architectural complexity; archeologists say its unique layout was designed as an ancient observatory of the heavens. Hundreds more ancient ruins are spread across the state.

But I don't have to visit these places or even study them to know that they're here. The ancient Indians are in the spirit of the land, and I can feel them simply by closing my eyes nearly anywhere in the region. It feels as if a group of wise old Indian ancestral beings are watching over this region and protecting it, nurturing it, guiding it ... and whispering to us all to let us know they are here.

I was not particularly intuitive in my younger years, but for some reason I've always been sensitive to the spirit of *landscapes*. Just out of college I took a job as a soil scientist for the US Department of Agriculture making soil maps in Vermont. My job was to hike the rich green landscape of that state, make notations on a map as to the soils I observed, and combine those later into published maps that farmers, foresters, and even engineers used. I loved that job, and not just because Vermont was such a pretty state. I loved it mainly because, as I spent day after day hiking the areas and studying the landscapes, I *merged* in a way with the landscapes.

And in doing so, I gained a sense of an underlying cultural energy, one nearly as tangible as the spirit I just described in New Mexico. In New England, however, my sense was of a wise old Robert Frost–like poet soul watching over the area and guiding its cultural integrity. I sensed it in the land, in the settlements, and in the character of the generations of people who lived there. I suspect many other areas of the world have those same cultural spirits supporting and defining their sense of place.

Introduction to the Higher Self

I don't think these culture-rich spirits underlying life are limited just to *landscapes*. I think every *person* has access to his own inner spirits, ones that guide him and support him throughout his life.

For example, a few years ago, as silence started to infuse itself more into my day-to-day life, I started to sense an intelligent *presence* inside my own silence. It was as if a wiser and nobler me were expressing itself in my thoughts and actions. It was almost as if, in a symbolic way, an old grandfather who was all-knowing, trusting, and loving was moving in as part of my identity. At those moments, my inspirations were deeper and more profound. Also at those moments, my path or purpose became clearer. Later, I realized what I was sensing was my higher self. But that term takes some explanation.

I'd known about the term *higher self* before, as a concept, but I'd never really understood it nor directly experienced it like this. As it moved in, I came to find that it was a wonderful asset to have in my awareness. It's definitely a very good thing, as it gave me strength, courage, compassion, and insight. I concluded that it represented the growing wisdom of my personal life that comes with growing silence. It is, in fact, most likely the source of my growing day-to-day intuitive guidance. But what is this thing called the higher self, and where does it come from—what does it really mean?

After much study, I feel I do know what it is. However, I also feel it's really not necessary to understand this concept of the higher self to advance in simple awakening. And explaining it takes this book in an even more spiritual direction. Because of all that, I debated whether to include a chapter on it in this book.

But it *is* a useful concept. It relates directly to the material on intuition I just covered in a previous chapter. And it relates directly to the idea that we all have a destiny and purpose in this life. It also helps present a cosmological framework that's useful when talking about awakening. So for all those reasons, I think it's helpful to discuss.

ABOUT THE HIGHER SELF

The concept of the higher self is something that not all teachers or movements of awakening talk about. For example, through all the years of the basic and advanced training I had in TM, I never once saw the term *higher self* mentioned. Nor is it mentioned in most other books on awakening.

But that said, the idea of the higher self has been discussed in *some* spiritual and even psychological writings for decades, centuries even. Its meaning has become a bit vague because the term has been tossed about in different contexts, particularly in more recent New Age writings. However, once you start advancing toward simple awakening, the meanings I relate below will probably become clearer and clearer.

Recall in Chapter 3, I defined the experiences of true awakening as being a shift of your identity from the small self to the larger Self. So a simple definition of the higher self is that it's that larger Self—the larger *you* that's based in pure silence.

This is not a bad definition, but it calls into question the definition of silence. If pure silence is, as I stated in Chapter 2, the unmanifest potential underlying *all* reality, how can it have an individual personality? How could one individual have a higher self that is different from another individual's higher self? Shouldn't they all be the same undifferentiated field of pure potentiality?

This may seem like a subtle or academic point, but it's an important one. Really, it speaks to the continuum of the cosmos—how the cosmos ranges, at one end, from our 3-D world of dense individual pieces of solid matter that our human bodies are made of to the other end, which is the unmanifest pure silence from which everything springs. There's a continuum between those two extremes, and the individuality and uniqueness of each person's own higher self exists somewhere in there, albeit, closer to pure silence.

So the best definition of the higher self is that it's the mostly hidden aspect of you that sits closer to the positive source of all life but that contains fundamental expressions of your individuality.

I realize that definition is fairly general, though, so let's explore it a bit more.

HIGHER SELF IN PSYCHOLOGY

The concept of the higher self, under various names, has been recognized in Western psychology for decades. Carl Jung recognized its existence, calling it the Self. Roberto Assagioli, a contemporary of Jung and Sigmund Freud in psychology, also recognized it and founded a branch of psychology around it called Psychosynthesis. A recent therapeutic approach called Internal Family Systems Therapy recognizes a similar concept. Transpersonal Psychology is another Western psychology branch that embraces the concept. In all these disciplines, the higher self, usually simply called *self*, is recognized as a central positive and wise subconscious force in our lives that we can refer to for grounding and guidance.

HIGHER SELF AS THE SOUL

In spiritual writings, the higher self is often also referred to as our *soul*. Now, the term *soul* probably has more definitions than even the term *awakening*. But usually, soul is described as that timeless aspect of you that exists, spiritually, above and beyond your surface-level projection into this earthly plane. It's commonly understood that your soul holds the spiritual essence of who you are. The soul is known to hold all your highest goods, aspirations, and intentions. And the soul can be accessed by looking inward so that you can gain guidance about your highest purpose for your life on this earth. For example, we use expressions such as "deep in my soul, I know this is right" or "this was a soul-based desire."

If you believe in reincarnation, the higher self, or soul, is that aspect of you that continues from life to life. It holds your lessons learned from prior lives, as well as your highest aspirations for future lives. It's your spiritual essence, which continues through all your incarnations.

ACCESSING THE HIGHER SELF WITH INTUITION

Nearly all descriptions of the higher self (and soul) hold that it's like the submerged part of an iceberg—it's the transcendent but more substantial portion of who we are. The higher self represents the best of who we are—and apparently, the best of us is usually hidden!

But that doesn't mean we're working with a less-than-full deck, because we have access to the higher self through our intuition. Our intuitive insights, which in the previous chapter I said we receive from silence, actually come to us *through* our higher self. So the higher self serves as our bridge with pure silence in our day-to-day life.

But it does more than that. The higher self also serves as the storehouse of our life's plan. As I said, our highest good and our highest intentions live in our higher self. Our inner wisdom and broader perspectives live there too. Before we are born, I believe we exist as a soul on the other side, and from that perch, we plan our forthcoming lives. After we're born, the higher self, or soul, subsequently attempts to guide us toward that plan in our busy and distracted world. When we get a deep-seated feeling or knowing about what we should do, it comes from there, from our higher self, our soul. Furthermore, the higher self serves as the storehouse of all our *experiences*. Everything we do and experience is stored there, even experiences from past lives, should you believe in that concept. How all those experiences relate to our master plan and how our plan gets updated with respect to those experiences—that all gets processed in our higher self, unconsciously.

One way to look at this graphically is to show this picture I drew years ago of the higher self sitting between pure silence, or source, on the left, and our outer small-self life, at the very tip to the right (see next figure). In this picture, the higher self is our bridge to the infinite, to the source. It encompasses all our subtler and source-driven existence.

Interestingly, the well-known psychic and spiritualist Edgar Cayce, in the mid 1900s, drew a picture very similar to this. He said we all are projections of pure source energy, which he also called God. He said that for most of us, life is lived only at the very tip of this projection, and we sit there mostly unaware of the vast support we have deep within us.

When I saw that description and picture, I was deeply moved that my own intuitive graphic was in some way confirmed.

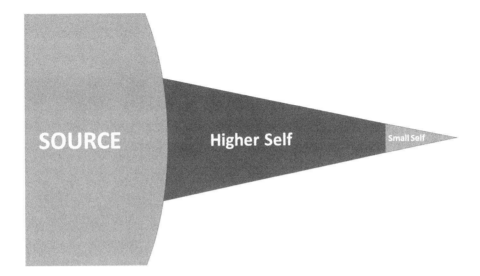

SOURCE   Higher Self   Small Self

With growing awakening, we activate the higher self in our outer, small-self life. With awakening, it's as if the higher self merges more and more into our daily life; it becomes an active player in it. That certainly describes the experience I've had. Recall the experience I described near the beginning of this chapter, where I sensed an intelligent *presence* inside the silence that was growing in me—that sense describes the higher self merging in. It was as if a wiser and nobler me were expressing itself in my thoughts and actions. At this point in my path of awakening, it's still somewhat indistinct. It's always there, but it's hard to put my finger on it and describe it. Presumably, with later full awakening, a full merging will result. Some say that with full awakening, with full enlightenment, memories of all your past lives come to your surface awareness. I'll let you know if that happens!

A COSMIC PURPOSE OF LIFE PRIOR TO AWAKENING

Now, you may think it's not fair that prior to full awakening we are somewhat or mostly unconscious to our higher self and that we can only access it indirectly, through our intuition, if at all. Referring to the drawing above, it may seem unfair that we have to operate in virtual ignorance, out at the tip of that three-part cosmology, cut off from the bulk of who we really are.

But in reality, working out at the tip, as we do now even *without* conscious contact with the higher self, has advantages. It's not a cosmic mistake that we're cut off. If we had full memory of all our experiences (especially past-life experiences), we'd come into this life with too much baggage. Many books have been written about this *amnesia factor* and how useful it is for us to get a fresh start with each lifetime. We are allowed to approach life with new wonder and a new sense of exploration—so it's a good thing.

Let me describe another reason, from another perspective, why not having full access to our higher self is partially a good thing. The writer Esther Hicks, who writes about the law of attraction and connecting to our true source, states the following about this (I'm paraphrasing):

We as small-self individuals are like an astronaut out on a spacewalk. We are extended out in space on a thin umbilical cord from the larger spacecraft, and that spacecraft is also extended far away from the whole of the earth connected only by radio. Because of that distant travel away from Earth, the astronaut is discovering things never known on Earth and so is adding to his knowledge and to the knowledge of mankind. But of course it's scary out there, floating away from our source.

This is an excellent analogy. The space walker represents the average disconnected and unawakened individual. The spaceship represents our higher self. And Earth in this analogy represents the source. Due to our lack of full connection to who we really are, we thrash about and make mistakes. But the disconnection also encourages us to try new things, to search through life for meaning and expansion. In that search, and in those mistakes, we make discoveries about the world and about life. We create new perspectives, and hopefully, we build character in our personality. Those new perspectives and enlarged personalities improve our selves and add to the greater collective consciousness.

For example, most of the work I did developing methods of time management, I did a decade ago when I personally felt as if I were failing at work. I worried that I was not productive enough. So in that fearful state I was motivated to create a system that later helped tens of thousands of people succeed in their own work.

As another example, Andy Grove, the CEO of Intel, used to say that only his ongoing paranoia about Intel's competition was what motivated him to keep innovating so rapidly. It's hard to conclude that Intel's innovations are a bad thing. Of course, one could say that corporate and even government paranoia has gone too far and is hurting the planet, and that's probably true. These days it feels as if it's way out of balance. However, as I discuss in the next chapter, I feel we will soon see a groundswell of connected individuals in leadership positions that will help pull that back in the right direction.

So disconnected action can be good and bad. From a positive side, it can be said that right now, having generations of disconnection is how it's supposed to be—that is part of the master plan to expand the diversity of the manifest world. In other words, from one perspective, it's not a cosmic error that most individuals are disconnected and bouncing around life a bit wildly right now. Rather, it's part of the cosmic design to increase the diversity and richness of the whole.

But no one can look at the war and suffering in this world and feel good about it. So it's also part of the cosmic design and the cycles of the universe that we eventually learn how to reconnect, to awaken, to contact our higher self, and to use that broader and wiser perspective to correct those problems. In so doing, we bring all that we've learned in our character-building dance with the world and merge it back with the higher aspects of our self. When that happens, we expand back into our higher self and back into the greater whole. Ultimately, that's the purpose of awakening.

In Closing

In Chapter 1, I discussed the practical impacts of growth of awakening. In this chapter, I've raised the discussion of awakening to a more spiritual level, discussing how it helps us merge with our soul and achieve our soul's mission in life. In the next chapter, I want to bring the book back to a practical level and discuss how awakening can help you achieve outcomes.

8.

AWAKENING AND ACHIEVING OUTCOMES

What does all this discussion about awakening have to do with the way we act and achieve in the world? Can awakening even improve our business lives? Let's talk about that.

My move to New Mexico has dominated my outer life for the last year, and I reflect on it often. Moving here has helped me write books and inspired me to create new work management methodology. In many ways, I have the ideal *profession* for living in Santa Fe and New Mexico because I can write my books and create my training materials *here* and then sell them *elsewhere*. I can easily fly from here to any other state to give my seminars. As a result, I don't need local sales to earn my living, and that's *good*. That's good because the qualities that make New Mexico so charming—its slow pace and its timeless nature—also make it a difficult place to make a living. The fast-paced business world has mostly passed New Mexico by.

There are pockets of business, of course. The northwest corner of New Mexico has numerous oil wells and related industry. Albuquerque, in the north-central part of the state, has a diverse economy and is very busy. There are a few more spots of business and especially government and military activity elsewhere in the state: Santa Fe as the state capital, Los Alamos Laboratories for weapons and energy research, White

Sands Missile Range to test some of those weapons, a number of military bases, and more.

But actually, these represent just small patches sewn into the fabric of a massive state. In reality, 95 percent of the state is just … *empty.* Even large-farm agriculture, as in the planting of wide stretches of row crops, is relatively rare here because there's too little water to support it. You only see row crops here and there, and only in small fields immediately adjacent to the few rivers that flow year-round in this desert environment. No, the primary experience of New Mexico, once you drive just a few miles outside any of the few cities and settlements, is that you're in vast expanses of open, unpopulated, and undeveloped high desert and mountains. And I *love* that.

The reason I love it is that as I drive the back roads of New Mexico, the vastness of open space seems to resonate with the vastness of the silence I now feel inside my being every day. The state's unbounded expanses are almost an outer confirmation and reinforcement—an *enhancement,* even—of my own inner unbounded experiences. It's as if having nothing mile after mile but natural and unspoiled surroundings enter my outer senses facilitates my own *internal* doors of perception to become vast and open themselves.

I talk about this because, as a result of spending time and traveling many miles here, I've learned how to accept and merge more with the natural rhythms of reality and less with the *man-made* ones. I'm learning that if I look to the self-inspired and self-activating forces of this unspoiled land, I find that my own activity can be more and more governed that way.

And that's an important lesson. One of the things I see so often in the business world these days, and even in many people's personal lives, is the unfortunate brute-force approach most are using to reach success. There's no natural rhythm in the majority of work and life these days. Rather, businesses and people seem to pounce on their goals with a vengeance, as if trying to *pound* them into place. Their ever-expanding money goals are demanding more and more effort, time, and energy to bring them into reality, and so more and more people feel as if they're slipping behind.

As a result, business and personal life in this country are being approached at a near *desperate* pace. Business leaders and workers seem to live in fear—fear of not meeting their money goals, fear of not maintaining their living standards, and fear of not keeping up with others' expectations, whether they be real or imagined. And nearly everyone I know who's trying to get ahead in the business world and in careers is living frantically—and *suffering*.

But it doesn't have to be that way. One lesson of simple awakening is that there are ways to achieve outcomes without constantly *forcing* them into place. There are ways to pay homage to the natural rhythms of your inner nature while you achieve the outcomes you want in your outer life.

THREE APPROACHES TO ACHIEVING OUTCOMES

In my 2010 book, *Master Your Workday Now*, I introduced the idea of the Workday Mastery Pyramid (see next figure). It's a graphical way to show three fundamental levels of work approach. While clearly I was focused on work when I wrote that, the pyramid is also useful for talking about living life in general, and even about *awakening*. That's because the pyramid can be used to describe how and why awakening is really the highest technology mankind has to advance toward personal and *material* goals.

Connecting
Your Work with
Who You Really Are
Connect

Creating Your Outcomes
by Using Now Goals,
and Goal Activation
Create

Getting Control of Your Workday
by Managing Urgency Zones
Control

Each level of the three-level pyramid demonstrates core work-and-life principles that are distinctly different from the other levels. Needless to say, awakening belongs in the top level. Discussing that level and the other two is extremely useful for showing why awakening is so essential for accomplishing outcomes. Let's do that now, starting at the base of the pyramid and working up.

THE FIRST OF THREE LEVELS: CONTROL

At the base of the pyramid is the *Control* level. It represents those strategies and actions we take to meet our ends by *controlling* our life, the lives of others, or things in the world around us. It applies to all kinds of work, business, and action. It's the method nearly everyone uses to try to achieve outcomes.

Examples of this level abound. In the direct-production businesses (farming, mining, manufacturing, etc.), control is exercised primarily through manipulation of nature and its raw materials. In organizations like business, government, and the military, control is exercised through the command-and-control management structures put in place to achieve organizational objectives. And in self-management strategies like time management, control represents the disciplines individuals structure to prevent wasting time and to encourage taking high-priority action.

You might say that the control level represents brute-force pathways to reach your intentions. Here's what I mean by that.

Let's say you're a company that wants to enable access to the raw minerals on the other side of a mountain. The main way to do that is to carve out a roadway around the mountain, dig a big hole in the mountain, and extract the materials. So you set your intentions, apply force, and get it done. There's no subtlety to this—you see the job and act on it.

What if you're a company that wants to increase sales? You plan a formal advertising campaign, deploy the advertising troops, and just do it.

What if you're an individual who wants to get a stack of reports written by the end of the month? You figure out how much time each one takes, schedule the time on your calendar, and then discipline yourself to work on them (and nothing else) during that allotted time.

So control is usually about taking step-by-step actions to reach an end. But it's also about holding the *discipline* needed to ensure those steps happen. That discipline usually takes the form of limiting divergence from your intended outcomes. So once a course of action is in motion, control steps are often *restrictive* in nature to ensure you and others stay on track.

You may notice that control represents the primary strategy of business, government, and personal work progress these days; it's been our primary strategy since the end of the Dark Ages. It's hard-nosed, it's practical, and it's action oriented.

However, the management approaches of control rely mostly on low-level human emotions like fear, shame, guilt, and greed, though they can occasionally also employ pride and courage. But because mostly low-level tools and emotions are used, control is quite limited in its outcomes. It ignores the subtler skills in life that are so fundamental in advancing ourselves and society in bigger ways. To be successful and create outcomes for individuals, businesses, and organizations, many more tools need to be used. You'll see what I mean by that as I talk about the next levels.

THE SECOND LEVEL: CREATE

What if the minerals in the mountain are just too expensive to get to—what if obtaining them just isn't practical? Or what if a market is saturated and advertising doesn't lead to increased sales? And what if you just can't get inspired to write those reports due by the end of the month? In all these cases, control breaks down as a primary strategy for moving the ball forward and reaching results. The old joke "the beatings will continue until morale improves" comes to mind to describe how control alone is usually not sufficient. Simple ready-aim-fire strategies quickly give out, and instead, you need to rise above those brute-force approaches to reach success.

That's where the second level, the *Create* level, comes in. It represents things we can do—that we have to do—to lead us outside of our stuck or limited world. It's the intelligence and creativity we use to think outside the box and to create new boxes to succeed in. It's the imagination we use to dream up and manifest new visions that expand our world and that break through impasses. It's the emotional intelligence we use to inspire ourselves and others, to positively motivate action.

As you'll see, this level rises above the brute-force action and management tools of control to reach progress. It employs higher levels of human emotion like trust, optimism, enthusiasm, understanding, and even joy.

This level encompasses an enormous range of methods. When describing this level in *Master Your Workday Now,* I limited my focus to tools that help you envision powerful goals and bring them to fruition. I described ways to write effective vision statements and essentially *will* them into place. But there's much more to this level.

This *Create* level also represents all strategies in work and life that require a bit of magic and that go beyond step-by-step action. For example, there's no step-by-step formula for creativity, and there's no guidebook for engendering inspiration. There's no manual for thinking outside the box. For individuals to succeed at this level, the power of imagination, positive thinking, and more is needed. This level is the level of alchemy, of mixing untried combinations of resources together to create new and creative outcomes.

A wide range of soft skills is included in this level. I mentioned above that trust is common at this level, and let's use that as an example. About a decade ago, Stephen M.R. Covey wrote a book called *The Speed of Trust.* In that book, he brilliantly describes how trust is an often unappreciated but extremely key factor in business, both inside and outside the company. With trust in place, business deals flow more smoothly and actions are made with integrity and autonomy. Without trust, the gears of business grind slowly, as every transaction is heavily controlled or second-guessed, which tends to gum up the works. The subtle yet powerful influence of trust is an excellent example of ways we commonly rise above control in successful endeavors in today's business world.

There are many other soft skills we take for granted that go well beyond control. The tricky business of finding or developing talented and creative leadership who know how to inspire workers is important. Encouraging entrepreneurship inside the company is also important.

The *Create* level is also the level of positive thinking. Remember those sixty thousand thoughts per day I mentioned in a previous chapter, most of which are negative? Those negative thoughts often freeze our forward progress. In the create layer we use tools to turn those thoughts to the positive and thus change physical outcomes. That's basically what the law of attraction is: creating outcomes through vision and positive energy. Tools like this *are* widely used in many parts the business world.

For decades—centuries even—the United States has been a shining example of this level. While countries like Germany and Japan were known for their hard work, discipline, and dedication to accurate production, the United States was known for its creativity and especially its positive attitude. For some reason, it's in the United States that people like Dale Carnegie and Napoleon Hill and books like *Think and Grow Rich* have led to generations of proactive and positive business enthusiasm. The New Thought movement, which led to a wide range of positivity writings and even founded the term *law of attraction* over a hundred years ago, hoed fertile ground in this country through the subsequent century. It then seeped into all aspects of our work culture. That tradition of positivity has, until recently, been the hallmark of the United States.

Unfortunately though, the *Create* level also currently represents the upper limit of how far outside the standard work box most of us allow ourselves to go in the business world. While tools in this level are widely used in business, taking soft-skill training very much further is a bit too "squishy" for many business people. While leaders tolerate motivational retreats and similar, if you stray much beyond this, you're likely to be dismissed or shot down as too touchy-feely.

All that's too bad because these days, even this *Create* level has run its course and we need to move higher. Our positive outlook as a society is crumbling as government, business, and even religion no longer deliver at the next level. More and more, we're finding that these organizations don't resonate with our current needs, and they often even violate our rising sense of decent behavior. As individuals, it feels more and more as if success and happiness are not being delivered through the standard pathways. For us as a society to move beyond our current limitations, we need an approach that goes beyond the control and even the create layers.

THE HIGHEST LEVEL: CONNECT

That's where the third level, *Connect*, comes in. This is where we bring awakening into the picture. The *Connect* level is a powerful level that greatly raises the stakes and effectiveness for manifesting outcomes. However, this level can be challenging for most businesspeople to accept because it so greatly transcends common-sense thinking on how to accomplish our outcomes. The good news is, not everyone needs to embrace it. It's there for those open-minded enough to seize the next paradigm. And even a small number of people doing that can greatly influence society as a whole.

What's in this level? One definition is that this level allows you to reach success and happiness by having you *connect your work to who you really are*. That's the definition I used in *Master Your Workday Now*, and in that book I demonstrated how you can do that in very practical ways. I argued that connecting your work to who you really are meant identifying your core passions and core purpose in life. By doing that, you then enabled linking your current work or new work to those passions. That of course greatly energized your work, and it made accomplishing your goals much easier.

So the *Connect* level in that book was all about doing exercises for identifying passions, purposes, skills, and core motivations deep inside you; writing a vision statement for work and life that matched those; and then either lining up your current work or finding new work to match that.

In *this* book, the *Connect* level can be described in a similar way, but I take it much higher. First of all, notice that *connecting to who you really are* is also the simple definition I give for *awakening* in Chapter 2 of this book. But I'm now raising the concept of *who you really are* to a much more refined level than I did in my older book. From Chapter 3, you know I say that *pure silence* is who you really are, and that true awakening is the act of realizing that. That's essentially what Self-realization is, having your identity shift to being that pure silence and then working from it through intuition, per Chapter 6. So really, awakening could be said to be the essence of what the *Connect* level represents.

Of course once you start working from your intuition, then it's likely that the work you intuitionally choose will be closely linked to your passions. You'll enjoy the work and more readily accomplish it. In other words, you could say this book's higher definition of *connecting to who you really are* still reaches the same outcomes as more mundane definitions.

TAKING *CONNECT* FURTHER

Because the definition of *connecting to who you really are* as used in this book goes much further with awakening, that leads to changing how the connect layer plays out in your work life.

For example, the style of functioning that comes with action in awakening goes well beyond mere passion. In awakening, you aren't so much emotionally excited to do your work as you are quietly and irrevocably *guided* to it. There's no ongoing effort needed to keep the linkage in place between your work and your inner motivations. No positivity exercises are needed, no detailed planning is called for, no life-vision statements are needed, and no motivational sessions are required. Rather, once you're in awakening, action in alignment with your highest good is practically *automatic*. Your path plays out day by day, and you act and work along it, nearly without effort.

Really, the *Connect* layer is the *best* place to work from. It's the most effective, the most satisfying, and the easiest way to get results done that are ideal for you. Let me explain why.

It's the easiest level to work from because if your life path calls for certain results at a certain time, you'll automatically be inspired at the right time and you'll get the results you're looking for. You'll waste little time, and you won't struggle to find work or actions that are effective for you and your goals.

It's the most powerful level to work from because you accomplish the outcomes most aligned with your goals—you don't need to constantly undo actions that are later shown to not make sense.

For comparison, in the *Create* layer, a lot more work is needed to manifest the desired outcome. First, you must set a goal and then apply motivational and visioning techniques. You may then need to make similar efforts along the way to overcoming specific blocks and delays. And even then there's no guarantee the outcome will happen, because the timing may not be right or the energy may not be lined up adequately, which can lead to great frustration.

Of course, *Create*-level approaches are certainly better than a brute-force *control* method, which may be slow, exhausting, and ineffective—and will eventually wear you out. But acting from awakening, as in the top *Connect* level, is so much better than either *Create* or *Control*, because the paths to outcomes appear naturally when they're needed and you take the steps as needed. You are guided through life and live life in pure congruence with natural law.

WILL YOU LOSE THE SPICE OF LIFE?

You might think that with all this automatic guidance, you'll lose the spice of life. Perhaps you fear you'll feel stuck if much of life seems to come in a predetermined outcome.

Actually, the opposite is true. With awakening, work becomes an adventure, a pleasure, a joy really. And it becomes much more meaningful. Here's why all this happens.

First of all, the automatic nature of life means each moment is a new discovery. Rather than planning or visualizing all future actions to the point that they arrive as expected without surprise, life unfolds in a continually new and fresh way. So there's plenty of spice!

Next, establishing silence along with your activity changes everything in a very pleasant way. Imagine always feeling in sync with life. Imagine all sense of unease leaving life. Imagine always knowing that all is well in your life, in your actions, and in your work. That means work feels like a joy.

Finally, you'll likely find that outcomes arrive faster. That's because the time wasted on misdirected dead-end attempts goes away. Therefore, if the timing is right, the pace of life quickens as you move directly to each next stage of life.

MOTIVATION INCREASES

One of the outcomes of true awakening is that you realize that ultimately, all is well in the world. You realize that everything is in its place and everything has its purpose. You find yourself on your path guided by intuition.

So another concern might be that this will impact your motivation to work in business. Isn't business all about solving problems? Where would your motivation come from? Wouldn't you just sit around enjoying your happiness and not move forward in life?

Well, from a distance, not yet having experienced awakening, you might think that would be true. But in fact I found that once awakening started to set in, I became even more motivated with my work. My sense of purpose increased dramatically, and that led to my thinking up more actions that I could do to help fulfill that purpose. In fact, I found I had more things than ever that I wanted to do in my business.

It's just that the motivation comes from a different place now. It comes from a position of strength and connectedness rather than from a position of lack, fear, pain, or discomfort. And really, that's where your business ideas *should* come from; they are more powerful when they do.

Think of the larger context. You now have access to your higher purpose, and you're inspired by intuition to act on ideas that will help you fulfill that larger purpose. Isn't that what you should be doing in your business? And just because you fail less often and succeed more, that doesn't mean you'll be less motivated.

LUCK INCREASES

One of the outcomes of awakening is that luck seems to increase. I don't mean you'll start winning lotteries (though I suppose that could happen), I mean things will be going in the right direction for you unusually often and with less effort.

That may lead to a question: will people look down on you because you seem to be living with a silver spoon?

Actually, while Americans like to think they honor hard work above all else, really they honor luck just as much or more. The heir to a fortune that spends it in an honorable way is praised way above a working-class person working hard. The contest winner is applauded and envied. The newly independently wealthy secretary to an Internet startup is gushed over for having been in the right place at the right time.

We also honor a business executive or owner who does very little except to make decisions based on her gut. Think of the movie scenes of the relaxed leader, listening quietly to the ideas of her staff and finally doing nothing but making the decision from her gut. In other words, we deeply honor good intuition as well as hard work. Not just those with intuition trained by long years of work, but even the prodigy teenage businessperson who seems to know how to succeed from pure instinct.

Even our fascination with action heroes in movies is as much an honoring of luck as of skill. When James Bond calmly walks, uninjured, through a hail of bullets without breaking a sweat or messing his suit, we are mostly admiring the luck that seems to follow him everywhere.

My point is that the luck that comes with awakening is just as honorable, if not more so, than doing hard work. Being lined up with natural law is a very impressive achievement. And most people who reach awakening do so only after years of attention to an awakening path—and possibly decades or even lifetimes of hard work building their character and their balance in life. In other words, they've paid their dues.

INDIVIDUAL VS. GROUP

Everything I've been describing to this point in the *Connect* level is with reference to an individual. It's been about how your purpose *as an individual* becomes clear and your business life improves. But what if you work in a larger organization? Do awakening principles work if you're embedded in a company or government?

Well, the principles of action that kick in with awakening do appear to function best if you work with a fair degree of autonomy. That's so that you can respond, unconstrained, to your day-to-day inspirations. It takes a fair amount of independence to, say, update your directions moment by moment as intuition guides you. I was self-employed the entire time that awakening was rolling in, and that gave me great freedom to react to my changing perspectives.

In contrast, if you work embedded in another company, it could be said that you should be following the goals and priorities set by that company, not those set by your internal inspiration. And I admit, that could be an issue.

But if you *are* working in a larger organization as awakening sets in, there are ways to do both at the same time: work on tasks assigned to you by your company and work on tasks that help you achieve your personal aspirations. In fact, I submit that nearly all workers in organizations are doing that all day long to some degree anyway. I think employees at all levels find a way to blend the two together even in the most constrained job or career. You usually can find ways to meet your personal goals while meeting those of your employer.

That said, I predict that by the time you reach an advanced level of awakening, you'll be in a role where you do have quite a bit of sovereignty. I predict that you'll either be self-employed and/or own your own business, or you'll be at a fairly senior level in an organization where you have more leeway to set your own priorities. In my mind, sovereignty like that comes with the territory. That's because, as you start to awaken, you'll naturally seek the ability to make a difference. You'll intuitively sense the need for more room to maneuver or the need for a larger sphere of influence to spread your growing positivity and act on your insights. I predict that by the time you reach a significant level of awakening, through your intuition you'll have guided yourself to the ideal role within which to express your cosmic purpose.

AWAKENING AND LEADERSHIP

In fact, I hope you do end up leading a company or organization that you can guide to have large positive impacts in society. Imagine if leaders in most companies were on the road to awakening or actually in awakening—think of what that could do for the world.

Recall that as you start to reach awakening, intuition starts to guide you on those things that help fulfill your higher purpose. And recall that the source from which all our higher purposes stem is that field of pure silence that underlies all reality. That field can, in unfathomable ways, manage the interconnectedness of all our individual purposes so that they line up and serve the higher purpose of the cosmos. In a sense, your actions are guaranteed to be ecologically sound if they come from your higher purpose.

Think about what this means for businesses as a whole. If all business leadership were awakened and leaders led their businesses accordingly, then their negative ecological impacts would be mitigated. Resources would automatically be balanced across various businesses. Growth would be encouraged only to the degree to which it's needed for the world, and in a way that supports the natural resources of the planet and the people involved.

Now, I'm not kidding myself. I know it's going to be a long time before enough of our business or government leaders are awakened adequately to make a global change. But I believe more and more people are going to start having awakening experiences in the years and decades ahead, and that includes our leaders.

And even if we don't see that for a while, it's still good to think about the implications of awakening and business. Starting with your own business, if you have one, wouldn't you want it to be in line with the principles I mentioned above: ecologically sound, with growth at just the right pace and all your resources balanced? And wouldn't it be nice to know that the energy that you invested in your business, if it came from intuition-guided impulses, was the optimal energy and in the optimal direction? Having that be true for your business really is possible, and in a relatively short timeframe, once awakening starts to set in for you.

IN CLOSING

As awakening progresses, you'll find your mode of action shifting away from a control style, through the create style, and more into a connected style—a style of functioning where action is mostly guided by intuition. If awakening is gradual, you'll probably be using all three levels of action simultaneously to some degree, for some time. There will be times and circumstances where no inspiration presents itself and you do need to control your surroundings, with perhaps even fear-based action—say, to protect your business interests from a sudden intrusion. There will be times when you feel that setting and visualizing goals, per the Create level, works as the best way to move the ball forward. And there may be times when intuition will gradually insert itself, in a balanced way, and action will be mostly automatic.

If awakening comes quickly, the shift to mostly connected and intuitive action will be swift, and that's good. That's because the connected action that comes with awakening really is the best style of getting things done. It's the most effective, the most influential, and the most enjoyable. It requires the least effort and provides the most bang for the buck. And it's automatically nature-optimized. In our ecologically challenged world, that style of work may be the only way to save our planet.

9.

Breaking Some Myths about Awakening

There are many myths about what it takes to become an awakened person, and a lot of them are focused on behavior, dress, and lifestyle—especially lifestyle. I think many people are trying to assemble the awakening experience from the *outside* in. Many people mistake spiritual appearance for spiritual growth. Let me give you an example.

I'm a Sunday driver at heart, and no matter where I live, I love to explore back roads—a lot. Before I moved away from California, I especially loved driving the dramatic coastline of that state, and the convertible I had while there was the perfect car to do it in. Due to the long rainless season, it was easy to keep the convertible top open most of the time—which I did. In fact, after a while, driving anywhere with the top *closed* just felt *confining* to me.

So when I took my first drive across country to Santa Fe, I did it in that convertible. Within days of arriving in New Mexico, however, it was clear to me this was absolutely the *wrong* car to be driving around New Mexico in. There are more dirt roads than paved ones in this state, so getting coated with dust or mud is pretty common when exploring, and a fancy car looks crappy when loaded with mud. Many of those dirt roads aren't particularly smooth either, so the low clearance of a sports car is a liability. Really, an expensive new convertible is just out of place here among the dusty pickup trucks and SUVs that are much more common and practical for the area.

So at the end of my car lease, which coincidentally was a month after my first drive here, an SUV seemed a sensible replacement. But I still wanted a *convertible,* and the only rag-top SUV you can buy is a Jeep Wrangler. So I bought one.

Within weeks of getting it, I discovered that Jeep Wranglers are the most owner-modified vehicle in the world—and I had to join that club. First, I added a sturdy front bumper and winch combination to rescue myself from those unintended off-road experiences that I just knew were coming. Then I lifted the Jeep a few inches to give more clearance over rugged trails. Next, I added tall and wide knobby tires for the same reason. Then, when I arrived in high-altitude Santa Fe, I discovered I needed more horsepower, so I added a supercharger, a performance air intake, and new gearing.

By the time I finished, my Jeep looked twice as big and gutsy as stock, and my friends were calling it the Monster Truck. When I was all done, I remember one friend looking at me and my truck and stating, "Michael, clearly you're channeling your inner fourteen-year-old." He might have been right—I may have overdone it. But I love my new truck and I wouldn't change a thing now.

One day I parked the Monster Truck in a Co-op Natural Foods Store lot in Santa Fe to shop there, and I encountered a tall, long-bearded fellow getting out of an early-model Toyota Prius. Dressed in what I could only describe as yoga pajamas, he spent a long judgmental moment looking up and down at my truck, and I could just feel his disdain. It was clear he felt I was not displaying the politically correct vehicle for that parking lot. And clearly my truck was holding back the spiritual and moral progress of the world. Essentially, I was not displaying a dedication to a spiritual lifestyle.

Who decides what the correct spiritual lifestyle is, anyway? And where are they getting their information from? The idea of awakening or enlightenment has been featured in literature, movies, and the scriptures of many religions and philosophies for hundreds and even thousands of years. But which of those stories, religions, or philosophies are accurate? Are *any* of them?

One test is this: How many people do you know who have actually awakened by following a particular lifestyle? For that matter, how many of today's *leaders* of spiritual traditions are truly awakened? I think until recently, the number of both has been quite small. If that's true, our knowledge and techniques of awakening are being passed down by mostly *unawakened* people who repeat what they've heard or what they believe, not what they have experienced.

We romanticize awakening and the awakening lifestyle, which is understandable given how transformational awakening is said to be and how it has the potential to end suffering for those who reach it. But in that romanticizing, many have lost sight of some simple facts about it, focusing more on the trappings than on the truth.

So in this chapter, I want to challenge some myths about awakening that have developed over generations, which are being promulgated by various teachers and followers. These are myths that many have come to believe but that I feel are not true—and so do not serve us well.

Myth #1: You Have to Live the Life of a Saint to Awaken

Perhaps the biggest myth about awakening is the myth that you need to live the life of a saint to awaken. In the typical version of this story, you're told that to be on the awakening path, you need to live a life relatively free from material desires. In fact, you're often told that the life of a recluse or monk is ideal for spiritual development. You might be told to eat only vegan, abstain from alcohol and caffeine, or perhaps even be celibate. In general, you're advised to take on a rigidly restrictive spiritual lifestyle.

It's understandable where this false belief came from. If you look at most of the current and past famous teachers of awakening, they did come from a monkish lifestyle. As a result, many followers thought they should mimic that. Some teachers pushed that lifestyle on their students because they had known no other way of living; it's all they had to refer to and so that's what they assumed was a factor in *their* growth.

And followers wanted to believe that. In our Western focus on cause and effect, we like to point to *activities* that create outcomes. So often, in the movies and literature that describe awakening, the *activities of a spiritual path* are what they point to. That dedication to a spiritual lifestyle *must* be the reason for awakening. Plus, many people who are emotionally stuck feel that they need a big change in their lives, and what bigger change than to completely renounce their Western way of life?

But I'm the perfect case study of how that's not necessary for awakening. In the five years before simple awakening started to move in, I had no spiritual activities or lifestyle in place. I didn't meditate, I wasn't eating a vegan diet, I didn't live in a spiritual community; rather, I was focused entirely on my business and social life.

And to this day, other than my added silence sessions, I remain the antithesis of a spiritual recluse. I'm not on a vegetarian diet; in fact meat, including red beef, is usually the main part of my diet (although I eat only *grass-fed* beef, for environmental reasons). I drink beer or wine with many evening meals. I don't practice yoga; my favorite exercise is to lift weights, and I do that three times a week. I'm not trying to compete in a body-building contest, but I find that such resistance training provides the most wonderful feeling in my body and is healthy for me—so I've been doing it all my life. In fact, I can come back from an intense session of lifting weights, immediately sit down and take silence, and have the most blissful and inspiring silence session. So the trappings of a typical spiritual diet and exercise plan really are not necessary, at least not for me.

And I don't adhere to the typical karmically correct buying decisions. I've already discussed my fast-car fetish and my new beefed-up Wrangler. The latter actually has some practical reasons behind it: I love to explore back dirt roads and trails, and so everything I've done is for that purpose. But the point is that I'm not driving the environmentally correct golf-cart-sized hybrid or a Subaru Legacy, which in many areas seem to be the badge of honor for spiritual devotees.

In other words, if you believe my awakening story, then it's quite clear that a delicate spiritual lifestyle may in no way be needed for awakening.

Now that said, if you generally prefer and enjoy a spiritual lifestyle and feel comfortable with it, then go for it. I truly think this is a matter of personal preference and suitability for each individual. Intuition will tell you what the right lifestyle is for you, so follow how it guides you. I know people who feel dull all day long if they eat meat and that negatively influences their silence sessions. And I admire those who live by their principles to improve the environment and the world through thoughtful buying and lifestyle choices.

But don't kid yourself that a spiritual or "conscious" lifestyle is *required* for everyone who wants to get closer to awakening. In fact, even the most spiritually devoted monk can be obsessed with his relative status and the things he owns while in the monastery. I've heard story after story of the bickering and jealousy that run rampant in spiritual organizations over the tiniest symbols of self-importance. My point is that a spiritual lifestyle is no guarantee of improved spiritual outcomes. On the contrary, if a spiritual lifestyle cramps your sense of style and happiness, it's only going to make life worse for you. It's not going to advance you in awakening.

Living a highly *moral* life is also often associated with awakening. Many stories of the awakening lifestyle imply or distinctly state that if you're growing toward awakening, you should take on a rigid set of moral behaviors. Some of these behaviors are explicitly stated in the texts of whatever philosophy you happen be following. In other cases, they are merely implied; they are communicated in the culture of the spiritual group as followers try to imitate the outer behavior of their leaders.

Of course, moral behavior is a good and necessary thing, but it too often becomes a *Control*-level activity (see Chapter 8) with rigid and sometimes guilt-laden energy behind it, as opposed to inspired action. My experience is that as awakening and intuitive guidance start to move in, highly moral behavior becomes more and more automatic. But if you were to try to *impose* a rigid set of behaviors based on doctrine or a leader's whims, you could lose touch with the intuitive guidance that comes so naturally as simple awakening arrives. A true saint isn't one who has memorized all the rules of the organization and toils over them daily. A true saint is someone who is so connected to silence, to spirit, that moral misbehavior is almost impossible.

So don't make the mistake of judging what behavior is truly correct and what isn't by observing others or taking on their rules. The basic rules of morality surely are very good examples to follow if you need them, particularly before intuitive guidance moves in. But much better is the internally-guided moral life that comes with growing awakening. Don't *try* to live like a saint, thinking that such effort is necessary to advance.

MYTH #2: AWAKENING IS A STATE OF CONSTANT PERFECTION

If you've studied the writings by or about famous awakened people—the ones who get the most attention, like Christ, Buddha, and so on—you'll probably come to the conclusion that they lived a life of *perfection*. After a brief enlightenment experience, or even right from birth, life appears to have been flawless for them. It will appear that they made virtually no mistakes, that the smallness of life completely disappeared, and that all of their life was lived in a perfected existence.

Such perfection *may* have been true for great masters such as Christ and Buddha. However, I believe that *most* awakened people don't rise anywhere near the level of these great masters. They don't reach that level of *supreme* awakening. People in simple awakening still experience the benefits I list in the rest of this book as they fully establish silence— they truly are awakened—but they just don't walk on water, so to speak. While they no longer struggle with life, they do still *live* it and its imperfections, in a mostly normal way when viewed from any outside perspective. Perhaps because of that, you don't hear much about the average awakened person or about his life.

To say that suffering and striving end with awakening is true, but that really just establishes a baseline of experience. There's still a lot of growth above that baseline, and there still is a lot of imperfection to rise above. Even if fully established in what I called *true* awakening (Chapter 3), in which your core identity largely shifts to being pure silence, you still have an ongoing co-identity with your small self, and it's a significant co-identity. It generates the details of your daily actions, it represents your outer personality, and it defines how you interact with the world. Because the small-self experience is a human one, it can never be 100 percent perfect.

In terms of how this feels to you, your life becomes a *mixed* experience that fluctuates between your attention being on the perfection of the larger Self, and then on the mundane of the smaller self, sometimes alternating in degrees. The larger Self—silence—wins in terms of being your true deep identity. The larger Self also comes more to the surface during especially strong periods of connectivity that can flood over your entire awareness at times.

But your small self wins when interacting with the world, with your friends and family. And in those interactions, imperfect human elements can appear to dominate. I say "appear." Once awakening is fully established, you'll never again be rocked to your core by those interactions. You won't suffer from them. But that said, as a human, you'll still be *working* on your human imperfections. You'll continue to grow.

Ram Das is famously quoted as saying "If you think you're enlightened, go spend a week with your parents." There are several ways to interpret that quote. One is that he is saying you're definitely not enlightened if, while there, any typical family issues arise. But if that was his intention, I think he set the bar too high. Even a fully awakened individual will continue to develop as a human. Many current writers about awakening say that after their first major awakening experience, they then experienced periods of emotional issues when interacting with family or in relationships. Does that mean they had not awakened yet?

After initial awakening, you still feel cycles of needs for food, water, shelter, companionship, and so on, and you'll move to fill those needs. You may even observe periods of some frustration in your small-self personality if the timing of filling those needs doesn't match what your small self thinks it requires—these experiences stand in contrast to the more connected periods.

There *has* to be variability in experience because, unless you become a monk and renounce the world, you're always interacting with the busy world and subject to the vagaries of human existence. And that's a good thing—it enriches life to mix your divine connection to source into a full range of human experience. Even with such a variable experience, I feel it's still awakening.

It's still awakening because you have reached a baseline of being established in silence. You see, the dips into the mundane look like dips only when compared to the peak experiences. For example, in my case, the bottoms of those dips are way above even the best of my previous non-awakened life. Even when life feels overly focused on the mundane, the silence is there supporting me, along with an underlying knowing that all is well. And even at the bottom of those dips, if I look for it, the bliss is there humming in the background.

MYTH #3: THE GRAND-FINALE AWAKENING

Related to Myth #2 is the belief that awakenings usually come suddenly and then stay permanently. I call those grand-finale awakenings; it's a common story in literature, movies, and some scripture, but I don't believe that's how it happens for most people who awaken. Rather, most people who awaken do so slowly and gradually. That's because in awakening, a lot has to change in your physiology, in your nervous system, in your doorways of perception, and in your habits of thinking, and it normally takes time for all that to occur.

We want to believe the grand-finale awakening stories for the same reason we want to believe in fairy-tale love stories: we want to believe that in one stroke, everything in life can be made infinitely better. For example, in a love story like that, much of the story is about a couple falling in love and the drama over clearing away blocking circumstances. Then, when all is clear and they finally both recognize their shared love, they fall into each other's arms and a glorious engagement or marriage occurs—and the movie ends. It's implied that all is perfect after that.

What you don't see in those movies is what happens in real life: the ordeals and growth that the couple have to go through after marriage. You don't see them having fights, briefly falling out of love, and then maturing and integrating love into their life in a more practical but perhaps more mundane way. And wait till they have kids!

The same can be said about awakening. It's true that at the time of a first major awakening experience, when the contrast is dramatic and enchanting, life feels 100 percent changed. You cannot imagine living a normal life again. It's true that sudden breakthroughs like that can occur—I reported one in Chapter 3. And most awakening writers are excited to describe those kind of experiences.

But after that, the experiences of awakening will usually then come and go in fits and starts. The first major awakening experience is usually followed by a sense of falling back, and it may be a while before a resumption of strong awakening experiences recurs. While you can find some writings on this, most writers of awakening don't prominently advertise those falling-back periods. You can find it in the back chapters of some of their books, but it's not what they usually talk about. Perhaps they feel it's discouraging to describe them. Or perhaps they fear their authority as an enlightened leader will be challenged. Or perhaps they were so long ago they no longer think of them.

But you should be aware that such falling-back periods will happen for quite a while in the early stages. There are several reasons for this. First, the nervous system has to adjust and regroup, and that takes time. Second, our psychology needs to adjust. We can be so enamored with the initial experiences that we want to then reject the normal human and mundane aspects of life as being passé and no longer needed. But eventually, we need to integrate our humanity, and we have to come down to that level to do that. And third, as I stated in Chapter 4, the awakening process is subject to natural cycles that we simply have no control over.

In the early stages of awakening, those falling-back periods can be long and painful by comparison to the higher awakening experiences you may have just had. My first major falling back came about three months after my first major breakthrough, and that lapse lasted two months. During those two months, I was sure I'd completely lost any semblance of awakening, and the smallness of life felt crushing by comparison. But then the awakening experiences returned.

The good news is those up-and-down cycles continue on an *upward* slope—the base of each trough is higher each time. Eventually a baseline of awakening experience is reached such that you never fully lose the silence again, and you never again doubt your awakening. At that point, referring to the river analogy in Chapter 3, your feet are always on the river bottom and you never feel lost in the thrashing current again. For me that came about a year after my main true awakening experience occurred, and that was about three years after the initial strong sense of silence arrived. Other writers have said it was a decade before they felt it really stabilize. Of course, your mileage may vary.

But even when you reach that point of stabilized silence, you still continue to integrate the awakening experience into your human existence—the two continue to blend in waves of relative connectivity, and the experience matures through time. My impression is that the growth never stops.

MYTH #4: TO AWAKEN, YOU MUST ADOPT AN ANCIENT TRADITION

Another myth I wish to dispel is that a student needs to adopt an established ancient tradition of awakening to succeed. So many books on awakening emphasize centuries-old disciplines or teachings, and I think that adopting them is just not needed.

One reason old traditions are attractive is that they are so mysterious. The old traditions can feel exotic and they can tickle your fancy. Their divergence from normal life can be magnetic to those who either are bored with their usual life or who feel that they have never really fit in with the established crowd. Many people are attracted to old traditions because they seem romantic and distinctive. But I feel those are all wrong reasons to go for them.

There *are* some good reasons to look to the old traditions for your awakening instruction. Many of those traditions have been primary custodians of the awakening ideal, and they may be the only sources of teachers in your area. There's also a comfort and confidence to knowing that the teaching you're adopting is time tested—with hundreds or even thousands of years of time testing in some cases.

But while finding an experienced teacher can help, and while a time-tested pedigree can be important, awakening does not *have* to come from adopting something old. Clearly, awakening is a very natural thing and can come through many different channels, ones that ancient traditions may have nothing to do with or acknowledge.

In fact, adopting a particular old tradition may *delay* awakening for various reasons. Why?

First, the knowledge in many traditions has been modified over time in directions that can be actually counter to their original teachings. The emphasis in some current teachings on forceful effort during meditation is one such example. Just because a tradition is old doesn't mean the current teachings reflect the original oral teachings. It's amazing how much a teaching can drift, as each generation changes it slightly over hundreds or thousands of years.

Also, the currently active teachers in such groups may not be awakened. They may be teaching because they adopted the tradition with great hope in their younger years. But now, even though they are still not awakened, it's all they know to do for a living.

Furthermore, even if they are holding to their original form, many of those traditions do not make sense in today's world and can distract you more than help you. For example, the elements of many awakening traditions are based on monastic teachings. They were established back when monastic lifestyles were a perfectly acceptable choice in life. But most aspects of a monastic life do not fit well in our society anymore and can even cause stress if you try to force them into your lifestyle.

What's interesting is that the monastic disciplines of such tradition-al teachings may not even be core to awakening success; they may just be incidental habits left over from those traditional periods, and they may never have had a bearing on growth to awakening. Many tradition-al elements were established merely for social and practical realities present in their history—not because they were needed for enlighten-ment. Examples such as particular dress, diet, and social or leadership discipline come to mind, and there are many more. Such exercises may seem attractive to you because, perhaps, you *do* need additional structure in your life, say, for personal reasons. Perhaps you *do* need to improve your diet. But those elements of the teaching often have nothing to do with awakening.

Unfortunately, many of today's awakening leaders were brought up in such monastic lifestyles, and they live and teach them mostly out of *habit*—with no value added to awakening. Remember, an awakened teacher is not necessarily a perfect teacher, and so an awakened teacher's habitual focus on those practices could be wrong if applied to you.

Finally, the collective consciousness of humans has been evolving for thousands of years, and teachings that made sense a long time ago may not make sense now. A completely new approach to awakening may be the best one for this age.

So my main lesson is this: You can start on an awakening path from nearly any lifestyle, and only you can be the judge of which path is right for you.

All that said, many traditions contain gems of knowledge that you can learn from. For example, portions of the old writings of each tradi-tion are usually spot-on with regard to what awakening looks like and why it's so valuable. So if you wish to *study* them, go ahead; use your intuition and find those gems, and enjoy their descriptions of awakening. But you do not need to adopt their traditional approaches. Rather, live your own life on your own terms.

MYTH #5: YOU MUST TRY TO "LIVE IN THE NOW" TO AWAKEN

There's a popular notion that to awaken you must try to "live in the now." This often takes various forms, including instructions to constantly watch your thoughts, as well as instructions to reprimand yourself when you catch yourself spending time thinking about the future or the past. Unfortunately, these and other teachings related to living in the now are, I feel, mostly counterproductive.

When, decades ago, I first heard of practices like watching your thoughts, they seemed odd to me. I knew we all could pay more attention to what we are doing at any given time, but I felt I was already doing that enough. It seemed as if trying to be *more* present would remove spontaneity from my life. In fact, it seemed that constantly watching my actions would be a dreadfully unnatural act—that it would make me self-conscious and uncomfortable.

However, with growing awakening, the meaning of *living in the now* is obvious to me. Living in the now is not making an *effort* to watch or appreciate the present as described above. Rather, living in the now is a natural *result* of awakening. That's because the natural and growing experience of pure silence in activity automatically places you in the now.

From a philosophical explanation, this is because pure silence transcends time—by its nature, it's beyond time. So as you do things that stabilize pure silence in your awareness, you also stabilize and emphasize the *now* in your awareness. There's a witnessing quality of being identified with silence, and it's very much an in-the-now phenomenon.

But that is a rather abstract explanation. Another much more understandable explanation is simply this: with awakening, the present becomes more *enjoyable*, and so you choose to spend more time in it.

With my descriptions of bliss in awakening (Chapter 3) and with my discussion of unconditional happiness (Chapter 10), I think it's clear how your present will be more enjoyable. There's a consistent bubbling of joy that creeps into the background in awakening, and it can make nearly every moment a pleasure, should you chose to pay attention to it. And even if you are busy and don't pay attention, it's there in the background at all times—and that changes everything.

For those same reasons, awakening also takes away the small-self tendency to focus on the future or past—a tendency that we all have prior to awakening. Why, prior to awakening, do we tend to focus on the future and the past instead of on the now? It's mainly due to the consistent background discontent we all have when natural and internal joy is not in place. Whether we're conscious of it or not, that ongoing discontent exists in everyone prior to awakening. That's because when we are not connected to our source—to our core of pure silence—inner permanent happiness is not a natural thing. Rather, happiness is based on outside conditions that are always changing. We can't help feeling consistently disappointed with such an unstable present. Even when we think we're happy, we unconsciously know that it will only be temporary, so there's a part of us that remains dissatisfied, immediately looking for more.

Such discontent with the present then drives us to look into the past or the future for remedy. For example, we may attempt to explain that discontent by examining things in our past that have led to it, hoping that such examination will help us avoid repeating those same mistakes. Once we identify what we think were past mistakes, many of us then take great efforts to avoid situations that duplicate them. We may try to avoid certain social situations, certain emotional experiences, and so on. We may be constantly on guard against them. Or we might be consistently pushing certain types of thoughts out of our mind. Those avoidance behaviors may be unconscious, but they can build up and then dominate most of our present. Or we may create habits of *compensation* that then start unconsciously directing our outer appearances, like acting tough or acting happy even when we're not.

All of these habits force us to live our current life dominated by the experiences of our past. They cause us to heavily filter our present experiences—so much so that we never truly live in the now.

With a dissatisfied present, many of us keep hoping that the future will bring a better experience—we keep looking to the future with visions of that happiness in mind. Certainly, anything is possible in the future, better things can be achieved, and holding specific visions of future happiness helps lift our spirits. Remember the Fleetwood Mac song lyrics "Don't stop thinking about tomorrow"; isn't that the correct approach to life? Well, in comparison to regretting the past and the present, it certainly is. And creating a positive future vision is very much a create-layer activity (Chapter 8), appropriate to do at certain times.

But there's a difference between creating visions of the future to build a greater you versus *relying* on such future visions to deflect you from an unhappy now. Recall in Chapter 1, I described that much of my pre-awakening life was spent in striving for the next thing and then the next? Such behavior was often valued in the business world because it made me appear action oriented and always moving forward. But I did that because I *needed* the next thing in order to be happy. Clearly, I was not happy with my present.

All that changed for me with growing awakening. Because of the bliss and joy I've described many times in this book, even when just in the background, a deep satisfaction with the now sets in with awakening. With joy hovering either at or just below the surface at all times, the now is pretty darn good, and both regretting the past and relying on a happier future just goes away. That's the true meaning of living in the now. That's the true meaning of being present. And that's the true meaning of mindfulness. Living in the now is not an exercise that you actively *engage* in. Living in the now is a result—an *outcome*—that you enjoy.

Myth #6: You Must Defeat the Ego to Awaken

In the writings of many spiritual teachers, you'll often see a message implied that the ego is a bad thing. They say that it draws us off our path and pulls us away from awakening. In general, it's implied that the ego leads to great mischief. Because of that, some people on a spiritual path have engaged in an ongoing battle with their ego, thinking that they need to defeat their ego as part of their path toward awakening.

First, I need to clarify that by *ego* these writers are not talking exclusively about pride or an inflated self-image. Rather, they are talking about the *entire* self-image, what I'm calling the small self or the personality self. It's typically called the ego in spiritual writings. And yes, the small self, or ego, when disconnected does often make mistakes—sometimes big ones. But bemoaning that is like declaring a child to be bad because she makes common childish mistakes. It's *expected* that the small self will make mistakes when disconnected. Don't regret that.

Even with all its problems, the disconnected small-self ego actually *improves* us all because it leads to a broader range of life experience and an expansion of the whole, as I discussed in Chapter 7. Also, in our

disconnected state, when we don't have access to intuition for moment-to-moment guidance, the small self protects us from danger. The
fear it generates, if appropriate and not excessive, allows us to avoid negative circumstances, and it motivates us to work hard and build a career
that feeds us and our family. All that is needed prior to the connection
of awakening.

Also, the way the field of Western psychology treats ego is basically
accurate when applied to the small self. In psychology, a healthy ego is
described as useful and essential. In general, one can develop a healthy
self-image in the small self, still have some basic fears and concerns in
the world, and survive or even thrive quite well.

Of course with awakening, life with the small self is much better.
That's because once in awakening, the small self's role changes, and
it no longer attempts to provide an accurate explanation of the world
and how you fit into it moment by moment. That's a role it was never
equipped to do well. The small self ultimately fails in that role because
it relies on applying its intellectual and emotional models from past experience to navigate an ephemeral and unpredictable world, and doing that
will never accurately reveal the world's truth.

The result is at best mild frustration or confusion, and at worst an
existential disillusionment with life. Only direct perception of silence
through the eye of awakening reveals the truth of life—one not explained
by our small self. Once that's a consistent feature, you let your small self
off the hook, with a great sense of relief.

In awakening, the small self's role is merely to be our interface with
the world, at the level of the world. Yes, it's still part of our identity but
in an almost playful, childlike way, one that you no longer take so seriously. It has no huge responsibilities because our larger Self dominates

as our main identity. So the small self is free to explore and play in the world in safety.

My message then is don't demonize the small-self ego. Send love to it, appreciate it for what it is. And, of course, continue to develop your awakening such that the small self, over time, gains the guidance it needs to operate more and more positively in the world, with less fear and more connectedness.

And the idea that you can or must accelerate awakening by destroying the small self is just incorrect. Yes, there are times while on the path when it makes sense to remind yourself that the small self isn't the entire story of who you are, or even the main story. On the path to awakening, you need to *release* your primary identification with the small self; so doing studies and activities that help you do that at key times can be useful. Some individuals can get overly attached to some aspects of the small self and refuse to let go, and that's why such work is needed. But in general, allowing the larger Self to flood in by taking periods of silence is often enough to enable that displacement.

And remember this: with awakening, the small self does not go away. It's still your interface with the world, and it serves you well. So develop the small self in those years before awakening such that it's strong, psychologically whole, and well-functioning. That way, it will be a useful tool to use once awakening kicks in.

In Closing: When Is One Awakened?

When we romanticize awakening, we often lose sight of how simple it can be—we make it very complicated. In this chapter, I hope I've cleared up many of those myths about awakening, ones that may not have served you well.

My message is this: Awakening includes a lot of normal life experience, and your degree of awakening experiencing can still vary. But if awakening can vary so much, what is the absolute definition of an awakened person? Don't we need a clear definition so we know when to claim "I have awakened?"

Really, there's an infinite continuum of possible development here, from the first glimpses of inner silence all the way to a Buddha-like state and beyond; so where *could* you draw a line in that? It's like trying to delineate the line between end of night and the official arrival of the day. Is the first barely discernible glow on the horizon in the very early morning the mark that the new day has arrived? Probably not. But does the sun have to be at the top of its arc before we declare the day's arrival? No, that's not right either.

If you must draw a line, here's where I would draw it. I feel that if someone has incorporated inner silence, pure awareness, such that it can be sensed at least to some degree all the time, and if one has found that their core identity has shifted to that pure silence to a significant degree nearly all the time—that's an awakened person. And that's true even though the prominence of those experiences can cycle from moment to moment, and even though many mundane aspects of life can come to the foreground at times.

This definition is somewhat vague of course and subject to interpretation. And the problem with any non-absolute definition is that someone might self-diagnose and then abuse his self-declared status. But I think it's safe to say this about that caution: If your sense of happiness and success depends on *declaring* yourself awakened, then you're not there yet; your small self is still too dominant. My advice is to enjoy the benefits of growing awakening and not worry about whether you can declare yourself "awakened." Eventually, you'll find a permanent ongoing joy in life, and the question will become a moot point.

10.

UNCONDITIONAL HAPPINESS

While driving the back roads of New Mexico in the last year, I've noticed more and more that a deep and permanent happiness has moved into the core of my being. I initially started taking these drives because I loved the rich colors of New Mexico's rock formations, the stunning dynamics of the wide-open skies, and the vast expanses of the desert, all of which open my soul.

But during my year here, I've found that my joy in this activity has evolved, along with my consciousness. There is now no one place, no one type of view, and no one set of experiences in New Mexico that captures me to the exclusion of others. Rather, these days, nearly *every* impression seems to float on top of an underlying, unchanging, and very satisfying layer of blissful silence.

In a way, these drives are useful for enabling me to learn more about the nature of that silence. In my many months of driving the back roads of New Mexico, concurrent with simple awakening continuing to develop, this is one of the lessons I've learned: Silence underlies everything and brings a baseline level of happiness to everything. My drives have become a touchstone for tracking my growing insights into the nature of that happiness.

Of course, that background happiness is not just present in my drives, it's now there in all of life. I can see that the baseline of silence serves as the matrix for *all* experiences on top of it.

An analogy that came to mind recently is that pure silence acts like the pure receptive canvas of a watercolor painting in progress. If you've ever created a watercolor painting, or even studied one, you know that the brightness and luminosity of the colors within it come from the whiteness of the supporting canvas (it's paper really, in a watercolor) underneath it. It's the intense white background shining through the pigments that creates the intensity of the colors. In fact, the colors wouldn't even be there if it weren't for the white underneath; they'd just be a muddled mess.

In the same way, the brightness of, or happiness in, the things you see, experience, and appreciate in the portrait of life are only possible due to the underlying receptivity of pure silence. As silence intensifies, so does the quality of the experiences that it supports. Of course, when you realize that silence really is simply your pure human awareness (Chapter 2), this all makes perfect sense. Your awareness supports and makes possible all your experiences. So if the purity and strength of your awareness grows, then your experiences become more enjoyable as a result. If awareness becomes so vivid as to be a permanent presence in itself (as an all-time presence of silence), its underlying bliss or happiness becomes permanently apparent throughout all your experiences.

When that happens, the result is the onset of *unconditional happiness*, and that's a perfect term to describe this growth.

What does that word *unconditional* in this phrase mean? I have experienced that with growing simple awakening, my happiness has become less and less *conditional* on having certain things or taking certain actions—happiness is just there. Unconditional happiness really is the right name for this experience because it describes a happiness that is not dependent on conditions, events, or circumstances. That experience is one reason awakening to silence is so transformational.

I like to say that there are two types of happiness. There's something I call *baseline* happiness, which is the ongoing background state of your happiness, present and steady from moment to moment. The other is *variable* happiness, which changes with the pleasures or experiences in the moment. When I talk about unconditional happiness, I'm referring to the first, your baseline or ongoing state of satisfaction. With awakening to silence, a strong level of baseline happiness moves in that is not conditional on day-to-day experiences. The variable type sits on top of the baseline and still fluctuates with events, but it's no longer your core source of happiness. Rather, it becomes the icing on the cake, and it usually seems relatively small in comparison to your ongoing and deeply satisfying happiness baseline.

NOT WAITING FOR HAPPINESS

One profound way I noticed the arrival of this underlying happiness was that I one day realized I no longer had an ongoing background dialogue that said "when I get this, *then* I'll be happy." The word "this" in that dialogue refers to whatever I felt I wanted either in that moment, that week, that year, and so on. One day I realized that dialogue was no longer there—it wasn't necessary anymore that I look ahead to a future event or thing to be happy. Happiness was just there; it then became normal experience, and I felt I was no longer constantly seeking *things* to achieve it.

Let's be clear about this. It's not that I don't want certain things, or that I don't feel an uptick in moment-to-moment happiness when I get things that I want. It's just that I'm not <u>un</u>happy *without* them—my strong baseline happiness is not dependent on getting certain things or on having certain life experiences. Underlying happiness is there regardless of those experiences, pretty much all the time now.

In other words, I'm not *attached* to the outcomes of my day-to-day pursuits, pursuits that may succeed or fail depending on circumstances. I think this is what the Buddha meant when he said suffering is caused by attachment to the outcome of desires.

Life as the Search for Happiness

I want to get back to the idea of *conditional* happiness, what most people live in. I clearly remember my experiences of conditional happiness prior to silence being established in simple awakening. I was always seeking something that I thought would lead to my next level of baseline satisfaction. The smaller, momentary wants were changing all the time. They might be little physical needs, emotional boosts, new purchases, fixing temporary health concerns, and so on. That next thing I needed was in the back of my mind as being the thing that would make me happy but was not yet present. As I matured, those things became bigger things, perhaps life goals. But their absence and the search for them was still the primary motivator in life.

That ongoing search was needed primarily because happiness from gains and achievements was so fleeting. It's amazing how fast we lose the boost from attaining something; then we're back to feeling flat again, looking around for the next thing to boost our mood. And the pursuit goes on.

I also noticed that there were usually several *levels* of pursuit that were running in parallel, with a number of longer-term wants stacking up. "Stacking up" is a great description of this, because as soon as one item was reached and taken off the top of the list, then after a short celebration (if any), another "need" was there right under it, also waiting to be reached. It could be big things like getting a better car, a better position at work or in business, solving a longer-term health concern, seeing or being with certain people, and so on. Or it could be small in-the moment things—but the stack was always there.

Many times I forgot about specific items on the list of unachieved pursuits—I became so accustomed to their constant unfilled state that I didn't recall them individually. Instead, there was an underlying dissatisfaction in place, either at the surface of my mind or just below it, about how I generally didn't yet have the main things I wanted. So I required daily small doses of foods, purchases, entertainment, friend encounters, small-goal achievements, and so on, to enable me to experience some continuity of happiness on and off through life—all while I was constantly on the hunt for ways to fill my larger goals, hoping to increase my overall happiness.

Aren't Goals a Good Thing?

Now you may think, isn't that the nature of life—to identify things we want and then go after them? Isn't it *good* to have a number of unfulfilled large goals to pursue? Doesn't that energize us and motivate us to achieve more and to move the ball forward? And isn't that better than just sitting around moping or being depressed?

Well, first of all, if you're reading this book, I suspect you're well beyond the "sitting around and moping" stage of life. I suspect you have pursued significant goals and reached many of them, and you're busy in life chasing down many other goals. Some of you may be doing that in a relatively relaxed way, and others of you may be extremely busy at it. In either case, having such goals and targets is not a bad thing at all. It *does* lead to a helpful focus on activity. And it *can* lead to significant accomplishments.

The problem starts when those goals turn into a "I'll be happy when I get…" statement running in the back of your mind. It's a problem when one or more targets become a necessity that you believe you must have *before* you can be happy. It's having your moment-to-moment happiness being *dependent* upon reaching one or more of those various goals and wants; that's conditional happiness. Conditional happiness is when you're so attached to the outcome of each pursuit that you feel unhappy without it.

And that's the key to the *unconditional* happiness that comes with awakening to silence. In my experience of that, it's not that I no longer have long-term goals or daily wants—I do. They add fun and focus to life. And reaching them adds to the richness of life. It's just that my core baseline happiness is stable and independent of those. Those wants and desires, and their fulfillment—if and when I reach them—are enjoyable, but they're not the main part of life's happiness anymore. Rather, an inner baseline joy that comes from an ongoing connection to source, to silence, and from the resulting underlying bliss is the main and ongoing source of my core happiness. That's what awakening to silence brings.

Don't Many People *Eventually* Reach Happiness Anyway?

I'm now at a relatively mature stage of life, and one could say that most of my primary, traditional life objectives have already been met. I had a successful younger life with no major life-limiting traumas. I had two moderate-length marriages that were mostly successful—until they weren't and they ended—but I moved on emotionally and look back on them fondly. I had good schooling and an interesting and varied career with modest but adequate money. And finally, I started a retirement business that is currently bringing in a reasonable income. In that business, I'm doing what I enjoy: writing books and speaking to groups. So you might say these positive life outcomes are responsible for the general happiness I'm describing. But is that really why I'm unconditionally happy now?

Well, no. First of all, I haven't actually met all my life goals. For example, I should have much more money in my 401K account if I ever want to completely retire. And I still have a long collection of things to be owned and life experiences to be had. And at the time of this writing, I don't have a life partner and haven't had one for a while. In fact, not long ago I was freaking out about both those things: my low retirement savings and my unstable love life.

But with growing awakening, all that has now changed. Not the conditions—those are still the same. But rather, unlike before, I now don't feel a big gap without those things—I don't feel I *need* them. I feel completely satisfied with where I am. I now consider those things "nice to haves," with reaching them taking a background perch. That's what the silence brought in.

Now, you may say it's foolish to, for example, not worry about building an adequate retirement account. Of course I'm working toward that. But the key factor as to why it doesn't worry me *logically* is that in the last years, I have seen over and over again that my intuition is guiding me to fulfill life's needs as they arise.

And really, in my mind, having a reliable and trustworthy intuition is the *only* reliable retirement plan. Think of how many people had their retirement plans wiped out when the 2008 financial crash hit. Think how many pensions have been busted when companies or governments declared bankruptcy. Even with tons of cash in the bank, you can never completely ensure a safe retirement through conventional means. For example, what if a major health issue arose? I've seen complete and well-funded retirement accounts wiped out in just a few years by a tragic health event. In my mind, the goal of complete financial security can never adequately be met. Engaging an accurate intuition to consistently guide you to meet your needs is really the only life plan I fully trust now. That's a goal worth achieving!

THE ONGOING SEARCH

So the general happiness I speak of is not primarily based on having fulfilled life goals, life experiences, or life money targets. While many believe that those things are the sole means to happiness, they really are not. In fact, I see many people near my age, fully accomplished in life, who have plenty of money and everything they could possibly want but who still feel life is incomplete. And so they continue their search for more satisfaction. Even with what should be a fully accomplished life, they're still unhappy with the results and hoping the next step will bring that next major step of happiness. They had bouts of happiness as they achieved each goal, but now their target of pursuit has moved on. Perhaps it's now "I won't be happy until I move close to my grandkids" or "I want to move to a warmer climate" or "I can't wait till the politics of this country improves." As a result, one or more unaccomplished targets are still always dangling out there, preventing their true happiness.

The point is, without awakening, unhappiness never stops throughout one's whole life. Think of the many classic examples of this that you (and others) experience from birth to retirement. As a child, you eagerly await your next birthday or Christmas and the gifts they bring. As you grow a little older, you cannot wait until you're a teenager and have the kind of fun you see young adults having. You reach that and then you see the more mature fun and experiences college-age people are having, and you want that. In college, you see the money people are making and spending in their careers after graduation, and you want that—you feel that will make you happy.

Then you see people getting married and seemingly happy, so you want that. But you find happiness in marriage is still elusive, so you decide having children will fill the hole you often feel. Now you can't wait until the children are a little older and less of a burden day and night. Soon you can't wait till they leave for college and you can finally pursue some of the goals you put on hold while raising children. All along you've been hoping to make more money, to get that bigger or more prestigious home or car, or to fund a business—and the sequence goes on.

I could give more life examples, at length, but I'm sure you get the picture. This constant raising of the bar is what causes one to consistently seek for a later outcome that we think will finally make us happy. And this is the list of *big* things; day to day there are also many, many small things we're convinced that we cannot live without.

UNAWAKENED PURSUIT

There's a repeating conceptual structure to this ongoing pursuit, and understanding it provides a bit of clarity. My first clear insight about this structure came after a longish awakening experience that then dropped away briefly. As I fell back into the old way of operating and started seeking happiness in *things* again, the contrast became very clear. With that insight, I drew the following picture that seemed to capture the typical unawakened dissatisfaction experience. It's a simple line with some circles on it, as I show here.

Let me explain how this picture works. In my unawakened state, at any point in time there's always something next that I'm seeking. That is represented by the open circle at the far right, and it's usually a specific thing, big or small. The solid circle in the middle is where I currently am in my pursuit of that thing; that status is typically incomplete or even at zero accomplishment. The solid line to the left is my history up to this point with my pursuit of that thing. And the dotted arrow to the right represents the time or effort needed in the future to achieve the thing.

So for example, say the open circle at the far right represents a high-income self-employment business I've been wanting to create. The solid circle in the middle is where I am now, say, with a struggling fledgling business. The dotted line at right represents the gap of unknown work or events needed to finally have a high-income successful business. The solid line at the left represents the things I've done, or the time passed, since I embarked on this business venture.

That past history to the left may be full of regret (or just mild frustration) due to my failure to reach my open-circle target—it often is with many people. The dashed line to the right often feels like a longer distance than I can travel or a larger investment than I can possibly afford to get what I want.

The problem is, no matter how much progress I make, the structure remains in place. This or a similar goal always remains at a distance, and it's never where I am now. Even if I reach the goal, I immediately replace it with another one, and I'm left, once again, in the middle of that structure. In the above example, it might be that once I reach a high income flow, I now find that I'm working too hard and not enjoying life. The new goal is adequate staffing and more time off—and getting *there* is now the struggle.

So this picture shows that I'm living my life consistently either regretting the past or living for the future—or both. As you can see, I'm not living happily in my now.

The fundamental reason is lack of Self-realization. Unless you find the pure satisfaction of living in your true Self (pure silence), you're constantly looking for reasons that happiness is not there. And so you blame the mistakes of the past or the lack of completed future plans.

Different people have a different emphasis in terms of where they assign blame on the various points of this drawing. Some people are living mostly on the left side of the diagram, consistently regretting the past and possibly even depressed. The world is filled with such people, and I'm sure you've met them. They mope, they whine, and they often relive the past and its failures.

Others are trying to think positively and work at looking ahead to the future. If that's you, then you'll focus on the right side. You'll be thinking about getting to where you want to be. That's certainly better, and in fact, it's the definition of a well-motivated person. But it still leaves you living for the future all the time.

Also, the manner in which you live for the future varies depending on your social and economic conditions, and your relative unhappiness.

If you're in desperate straits financially or emotionally, you may be hopelessly scrambling for that next thing you think you need. That can be experienced as a state of constant frustration and perhaps even futility. If you're not too bad off or simply very ambitious, it may be that you're merely working very hard hoping to get ahead. While that may seem admirable, the trouble is, that goes on forever—I call that *constant striving*.

Or perhaps you're retired and the big work pursuits are no longer a factor. But even for the comfortably retired, I guarantee that unless you're awakened, you're still dominated by many "I'll be happy when…" statements floating in the front or back of your mind, even though you're surviving well and not working so hard. It's just that those statements are now focused on non-career topics.

DISCONNECTED ACTION

You may think, "Well, that's life—those ongoing desires are what move us forward and keep us improving ourselves and the world. And to some degree I *like* having these challenges."

The trouble with that statement is that the actions we take to fill our insatiable happiness gaps are almost always *disconnected* actions, and such actions usually have negative side effects. They then compound the complications of life and lead to more and more problems.

You see, when you're guided by awakened intuition, your actions are *connected* ones, guided by your life plan and ultimately by the universe, and so they are infinitely appropriate. But when your actions are *disconnected*, they lack that support and usually have negative side-effects. A simple example might be cutting someone off in traffic to get to the store faster, ruining their day and bothering yourself as well. But it might be on a larger scale, like an entire society so dependent on material gain for happiness that it consumes the majority of the world's resources. It might be polluting the environment in a business that states its lofty goal is providing jobs that enable people to buy more and more goods so they can continue to be happy. Or it might be conducting a war to protect the raw resources that feed the creation of those material goods.

As I stated in Chapter 8, it does not have to be that way. There *are* ways to achieve great outcomes yet keep your impact universally benign all along the way.

RESULT OF AWAKENING TO SILENCE

Awakening to silence makes achieving outcomes with balanced actions possible. The insatiable and desperate search for happiness ceases. That line-and-circle structure I showed above is replaced primarily with the single middle solid dot. While you honor the past and are warm to future prospects, your obsession with the past goes away. And your obsession with a gap you're constantly trying to close in the future also goes away. That middle dot, your *now*, takes on new meaning, new richness. That's because you're mostly living in the now, in unconditional happiness. Not only do you not regret the past, but you don't depend on reaching future goals or desires as your primary way to reach happiness. Rather, a deep richness sets in as you find ongoing happiness in the now.

IN CLOSING

What does this unconditional happiness feel like? Well, it's an underlying, all-time knowing that *all is well*. And that knowing remains there whether I'm sitting quietly and contently or whether I'm inspired to actively surf the leading edge of my life's adventure. No matter what

I'm doing, there's a deep unquestioning sense that I'll always be living what's best for me and for the world around me, and that I'll always be happy in the midst of it all. In fact, it's not even a knowing, it's a *being*. It's a state of consciousness. And add to that the surface or below-surface bliss that I spoke of earlier, a bliss that reaches every level of my being, and it's a pretty nice package.

AFTERWORD

It's been six months since I completed writing the majority of this book. I decided to put it aside for a while before I polished it up and sent it to press, primarily to let it percolate a little. I wanted to see if any new insights had arisen, and I wanted to confirm that, over time, the core message of this book was still the *best* message for me to convey. I guess I wanted to give it the test of time. As I look back on it now, I see no major changes that I need to make, but I do have some final thoughts.

First, I'm not sure I could write this book *now*. Why? Because, I don't have the *contrast* that I did a year ago, contrast that led me to be so expressive. In the last six months since stopping work on the book, my awakening experiences have become established essentially full-time—they've become a permanent feature of life. There are no longer any major dips or dropping away of awakening experiences that, in the past, led me to see the contrast in such vivid detail. So without that distinction, there's a little bit less to write about and less to marvel over.

And yet of course I'm not complaining. Awakening remains the most amazing thing I can possibly imagine. But the way I talk about it has changed somewhat. When people ask me to summarize it briefly these days, I don't talk first about bliss, and I even don't talk first about silence, although both of those are as strong as ever. Rather, the first thing that comes to my mind these days is the phrase "the end of suffering." That's because as I look around, I see so much suffering in people's lives, even in those who are successful and well-off. And I want to help solve that for them and others. So perhaps what is happening with me now is that I'm *maturing*. Rather than being so caught up in my own experiences, my *compassion* is growing, and it's causing me even more to want to help improve the conditions of others. And awakening is such an obvious solution.

In looking at others, the trouble I see is that most people are still desperately *striving*. They're still chasing happiness in an intense and often frantic way. They're scrambling to make their life, their career, their families—essentially their happiness—finally start to work. The desperation may be unconscious and below the surface, but its widespread presence is obvious to me, and to me it's a distinct form of suffering. Since even simple awakening brings the end of *seeking* as a base level of happiness becomes established, *the end of suffering* is to me the best way to describe awakening. So that's the first new insight I now have.

Another new insight is that I now see that this simple awakening is just a starting point. It's like removing shackles from your feet so that you can finally start walking forward. Rather than spending so much time and energy pinned to, and pounding on, the same limited means to find happiness, you're free from that now. With the freedom of awakening, you're now able and inspired to pursue bigger goals. New vistas open up that compel new movement forward.

For me personally, those goals and vistas are to explore and explain awakening so that others can learn it and find relief and expansion in life—through books I write, through teachings I give, and through who knows what else. For others who awaken, perhaps their goals might be developing new technologies that are based on consciousness. For others it might be a dedication to *healing*, either of individuals or the planet. So my other new observation, in the last six months, is that there *is* life after initial awakening. We often think of awakening as an end point—but it's really a *beginning* point, and you'll be very busy after you get there!

To conclude this book, let me say one more thing about my beloved New Mexico. As I continue to live here in Santa Fe and travel the state, the richness of this place continues to develop for me and in my awareness. Interestingly, the motto of this state—the one displayed on most license plates—is *Land of Enchantment*. I'm finding that my growing depth of silence reveals, even more, my connection to the depth of the enchantment of this land. The true culture of this land is emerging more and more for me, and it goes well beyond the adobe structures, the Indian jewelry, the old Spanish churches, and the other surface-level attractions that so many tourists flock here for.

Rather, I'm becoming aware that the magic of this place is hidden inbetween the lines. There's an almost shamanic undercurrent that is begging to be revealed. I've decided that the strong and magic spirit underlying New Mexico may in fact be one of America's last true connections to its indigenous and nurturing roots. Nowhere else do I see such dedication to a cultural heritage that can truly be called American. Nowhere else do I sense such a multilevel, even multidimensional, depth at the root of daily life. The fact that the big-business world has largely passed New Mexico by is a *good* thing, as it has allowed most of that old spirit to remain largely unspoiled. That perhaps gives New Mexico a special role.

If there's a profound and soul-based teaching that is going to revitalize and re-energize the disconnected and desperate lives that so many people in America live today, I do believe it may come from here, from New Mexico. If so, I hope I can be a small part of that. I hope that as I grow even more in awakening and connect even more deeply with New Mexico's richness, I can find new and powerful ways to enrich other people's internal lives, all from my perch in this enchanted state.

ABOUT THE AUTHOR

Michael Linenberger has held major roles in the field of information technology and business management for over twenty years. He is a former vice president at the management consulting firm Accenture; prior to that he worked as head of technology at US Peace Corps. An expert on managing work tasks and communication, Michael has written seven books on workday productivity, among them several best sellers.

Michael holds a BS in Soil Science and a BS and MS in Civil Engineering from The University of Massachusetts. He started his career in 1976 as a soil scientist for the US Department of Agriculture. In the 1980s, he worked as a civil engineer designing foundations for some of the largest buildings in San Diego, California.

For more than forty years, Michael has also been interested in the development of consciousness. He currently gives talks and seminars on improving business and personal life.

For more information and to sign up for Michael's free newsletters or blog, go to SimpleAwakening.com.